DIAMONDS FROM DANIEL

BIBLE STUDY AIDS *of William G. Heslop*

* Gems From Genesis
* Extras From Exodus
* Lessons From Leviticus
* Nuggets From Numbers
  * Rubies From Ruth
  * Sermon Seeds From The Psalms
  * Pearls From the Prophet Ezekiel
  * Diamonds From Daniel
* Gold From the Gospels (Matthew)
* Pen Pictures From Paul (Romans)
* Riches From Revelation

DIAMONDS FROM DANIEL

by

William G. Heslop, D.D., Litt., S.D.

KREGEL PUBLICATIONS
Grand Rapids, Michigan 49501

Diamonds From Daniel reprinted by Kregel Publications, a division of Kregel, Inc., under special arrangements with the original publisher, Nazarene Publishing House. All rights reserved.

Library of Congress Catalog Card Number: 76-12082
ISBN 0-8254-2833-5

First edition 1937
Kregel Publications edition 1976

Printed in the United States of America

CONTENTS

Key to the Book of Daniel 7
The Book of Daniel 11
The Times of the Gentiles 13
Analysis of Daniel 17

1. The Personal History of Daniel 24
2. Nebuchadnezzar's Dream 33
3. The Image of Gold 56
4. Conversion of A King 67
5. Drinking and Dancing 76
6. Daniel in the Lion's Den 86
7. The Four Great Beasts 93
8. The Vision of the Ram and the He Goat 116
9. The Profoundest Prophecy in the Bible 133
10. Michael the Archangel 152
11. The Coming Anti-Christ 159
12. The Closing Scenes 173

KEY TO THE BOOK OF DANIEL

The Second Coming of Christ is the Golden Key which unlocks the Book of Daniel. The Bible teaches the personal return of Christ to reign as definitely, simply, clearly and as unambiguously as it taught His first coming to suffer and die. The Bible teaches in plain language the actual, literal, personal, bodily return of Christ to this earth. There never will be peace on earth until the return of the Prince of Peace. There will never be a millennium of righteousness and rest until Jesus Christ returns. *Not until Christ returns* will injustice, inequality and selfishness cease. *Not until Christ returns* will the curse be lifted from man and beast. *Not until Christ returns* will righteousness cover the earth as the waters cover the sea. *Not until Christ returns* shall those who sleep in Him arise. *Not until Christ returns* will the groan be taken from the earth. *Not until Christ returns* will the bride and bridegroom immortal be united in holy marriage and celebrate the marriage supper of the Lamb. *Not until Christ returns* will He sit upon the throne of His Father David (Luke 1:31-33). *Not until Christ returns* will the kingdoms of this world be destroyed and the Stone fill the whole earth. *Not until Christ returns* will God's will be done in earth as it is done in heaven. *Then* and not until then shall there come a new heaven and a new earth, a new city and new nations, and sin, sorrow, strife, pain, death and war cease. All creation awaits the happy hour of Christ's Second Advent. The Smiting Stone is coming and from the depths of his unworthy heart, the writer cries "Even so, come Lord Jesus." Amen!

The Book of Daniel and His Critics

The Book of Daniel has been a veritable battleground for centuries. Carping, inconsistent critics both inside and outside of the pulpit have hammered away against this anvil upon

8 / DIAMONDS FROM DANIEL

which their hammers have been broken to pieces. Kuenen and Wellhausen with their inferior disciples of our own day have done their best to discredit Daniel and belittle the book which bears his name. They have all miserably failed. Their names will soon be forgotten while Daniel lives on, and his book blesses the world. As far as this insignificant scribe is concerned, the question of the authenticity, veracity, inspiration and authority of the Book of Daniel has never been questioned, nor even open for debate since he read Matt. 24:15. This should be enough for every Christian. Our blessed Lord, the infallible Son of God mentions Daniel by name in his matchless marvelous message delivered on Olivet (Matt. 24: 15). When our Lord uttered the words "Daniel the Prophet" he set his sovereign seal on both the writer and the book which bears his name. That the Book of Daniel was written and known before the advent of Antiochus Epiphanes is easily proved by remembering that the Septuagint or Greek version of the Old Testament, which was made before the time of the Maccabees, contains the Book of Daniel. The Book therefore antedates the time of Antiochus and gives one sure knockout upper cut to the critics.

Daniel, the Dissolver of Doubts

Daniel was distinguished for his deep piety, profound sagacity and religious consistency. He was skilful in wisdom, cunning in knowledge, an interpreter of dreams, a dissolver of doubts and of an excellent spirit. His heart was holy, his mind was pure, his body was clean and his spirit was guileless. As a seer he stands without a peer. He foretold the rise and fall of Babylon, the fearful insanity of Nebuchadnezzar, the death of Belshazzar, the rise, progress, decay and doom of the Medo-Persian empire, the coming of Alexander the Great, the Conquests of Rome, the apocalypse of the Anti-Christ and the end of the world. He read, at once, to Belshazzar, the ominous, startling handwriting on the wall. He was a profound student of the prophetic scriptures. He unceasingly prayed and untiringly labored for his God and His people. He lived through the reigns of Nebuchadnezzar, Belshazzar, Darius and at least through the first year of Cyrus and was finally assured by his Jehovah God that he should "stand in his lot at the end of the days." Daniel clearly reveals that the rise and fall of Ancient Empires were all preparatory to the coming of the Messiah. His predictions have been so minutely fulfilled, and so strikingly verified by subsequent history that some infidels and higher critics have been driven to despair and have alleged that the Book of Daniel must have been written after the events took place. The Book of Daniel is also full of cheering instruction. It shows that the God of the Bible and the God of Israel presides over nations, that He wields their destinies, changes the decrees of mad monarchs, exalts the holy, abases the proud and works out His own will despite the depravity of despotic kings and peasants.

Hebrew prophets were inspired instructors of the people. They were holy men speaking in God's name to men and nations. Whether they expounded the histories of the past, enforced duties in the present or revealed mysteries to come they spake for God and in God's name. In the darkest days God never left Himself without a witness. Daniel was not by any means the least of those prophets, instructors, seers and witnesses.

THE BOOK OF DANIEL

The Book of Daniel is the twenty-seventh book of the Old Testament, and contains twelve chapters. The book was written between 606-534 B.C. by Daniel whose name it bears. He prophesied during the whole of the seventy years captivity and now rests from his labours until the end of the days.

The outstanding evidence of the authenticity of the Book of Daniel is the testimony of our Blessed Lord Himself. He quoted from this book as recorded in Matt. 24:14, 15, 30; Luke 21:24 and again in Matt. 26:63-64. Thus our Lord clearly commends to us the reading and study of the Book of Daniel.

Author: Daniel.
  (1) Carried captive by Nebuchadnezzar.
  (2) Purposed in His heart to be pure even in the midst of impurity.
  (3) Honored by the God of heaven and the kings of earth.

Date:—606-534 B.C. From Nebuchadnezzar, King of Babylon, to Cyrus, King of the Medes and Persians.

Place—Babylon.

Chief Purpose—
  (1) To show the sovereignty of Jehovah.
  (2) The success of world-power is but temporary.
  (3) The Kingdom of Christ shall finally triumph over all.

The one great object of the Book of Daniel is to bring out the power of God. The Sovereignty of God is shown on every page of this profound book of Prophecy.

1. GOD'S POWER is shown in the character and conduct of Daniel and his three Hebrew friends.

2. GOD'S POWER is revealed in the remarkable wisdom displayed by Daniel.

3. GOD'S POWER is pictured in the dream of Nebuchadnezzar and the interpretation thereof by Daniel.

4. GOD'S POWER is declared in His deliverance of the true and trusting three companions of Daniel from the fiery furnace.

5. GOD'S POWER is set forth in his judgment dealings with Nebuchadnezzar. (1) Warning him. (2) Punishing him. (3) Restoring him.

6. GOD'S POWER is wonderfully displayed in the doom-sealing handwriting on the wall at Belshazzar's feast when the recklessness of Belshazzar brought upon him the retribution of God.

7. GOD'S POWER is seen in the deliverance of Daniel from the den of lions. We have thus revealed the power and presence of God in all the affairs of men and nations. He wrought wonders for His people when they were captives in Egypt and He showed forth his mighty power when His people were captives in Babylon. World Rulers were compelled to confess that the God of the Bible and the God of the Hebrews was the only true and living God, the Most-High Ruler in Heaven and earth.

THE TIMES OF THE GENTILES

The times of the Gentiles is that long period during which Jerusalem is politically subject to the rule of the Gentiles. It began with the Babylonian captivity of Judah under Nebuchadnezzar and it will end by the destruction of Gentile dominion by the Coming of the Lord in glory (Dan. 2:34, 35, 44—Rev. 19:11, 21).

There are three somewhat similar expressions in the Bible which ought to be clearly understood.

1. "The Times of the Gentiles."
2. "The Fulness of the Gentiles."
3. "The Fulness of the Times."

The first phrase "The times of the Gentiles" is used to designate that period of time during which the Gentile nations exercise dominion over the earth. *God told Adam* to "multiply, and replenish the earth, and subdue it, and have dominion." Adam lost that dominion through disobedience. After the flood God told Noah to "multiply and replenish the earth, and have dominion." The chosen race through Seth, Enos, Cainan, Mahalaleel, Jared, Enoch, Methuselah, Noah and Shem was thus given dominion over the earth. That dominion was lost by disobedience. Such disobedience culminated in the building of the Tower of Babel which brought the judgments of God in the confusion of tongues. God then called Abraham and through Abraham promised THE KING whose dominion would be an everlasting dominion. God's chosen race was to rule the earth. The disobedience of God's people brought disaster and dissolution culminating in the captivity in Babylon. Nebuchadnezzar, King of Babylon was the first Gentile world ruler to subdue God's people after their establishment in the land of Canaan. Nebuchadnezzar overturned the throne of David and carried away the people and the times of the Gentiles began. Such times will go on until the return of Christ as King. The times of the Gentiles will continue until the apocalypse of the Anti-Christ who will be the last Gentile World Ruler. Our Lord himself said "Jerusalem shall be trodden down of the Gentiles until the times of the Gentiles be fulfilled" (Luke 21:24).

The times of the Gentiles thus began with Nebuchadnezzar and will end with the destruction of the Anti-Christ by the personal appearance of Christ as King.

The expression "The fulness of the Gentiles" is altogether different. Romans 11:25 "For I would not, brethren, that ye should be ignorant of this mystery, lest ye should be wise in your own conceits; that blindness in part is happened to Israel, until the fulness of the Gentiles be come in."

Israel has been and is now hardened in heart and blinded in eyes and shall so continue until the elect number of the Church has been called out and completed.

Acts 15:13-17 "And after they had held their peace, James answered saying, Men and brethren, hearken unto me: Simeon hath declared how God at the first did visit the Gentiles, *to take out* of them a people for his name. And to this agree the words of the prophets; as it is written, *After this I will return,* and will build again the tabernacle of David which is fallen down; and I will build again the ruins thereof, and I will set it up: That the residue of men might seek after the Lord, and all the Gentiles, upon whom my name is called, saith the Lord, who doeth all these things." The purpose of God in this age is thus clearly set forth, (1) God is now visiting the Gentiles (The times of the Gentiles) (2) God is now taking out from among the Gentiles a people for his own name (The Church) (3) The return of Christ. After the return of Christ the Kingdom will be restored to Israel and the millennial reign of Christ will begin. The "fulness of the Gentiles" thus deals with the completed Church which began on the morning of the Resurrection of Christ and is to end at the rapture of the Saints.

The phrase "The fulness of the Times" which may be found in Eph. 1:7-10 refers to the eternal state when all things shall have been fulfilled and summed up in Christ.

To briefly recapitulate

1. THE TIMES OF THE GENTILES has reference to the dominion of the Gentiles.
2. THE FULNESS OF THE GENTILES deals with the calling out and completion of the Church of Christ.
3. THE FULNESS OF TIMES sets forth the eternal age.

ANALYSIS OF DANIEL

Chapters
1. The Personal History of Daniel............1 and 6
2. The Dreams of Nebuchadnezzar............2 and 4
3. The Three Hebrews 3
4. Belshazzar's Great Feast.................. 5
5. The Visions of Daniel.....................7 to 12

I. The Personal History of Daniel

(1) Daniel was taken to Babylon by Nebuchadnezzar in the third year of the reign of Jehoiakim, king of Judah. He was one of the children of Israel and of the king's seed who was chosen for a special course in the college of Babylon. The national sins of Judah had brought upon the race the inevitable judgments of God and Daniel with his three companions suffered captivity with the rest of the nation. Daniel came face to face with a real test to his trust in the God of the Hebrews during the first semester of his college career in Babylon. A daily provision of the king's meat and of the king's wine was one of the necessary courses.

Daniel requested that he might not defile himself while purposing in his heart to be true to God and God's word. After ten days of trial the countenances of the Hebrews appeared fairer and fatter than all other students. The first test was thus passed and God gave Daniel and his three friends knowledge and skill in all learning and wisdom.

(2) The second test came as a result of the dream of Nebuchadnezzar. The dream had stirred the despotic king and realizing the importance of obtaining an interpretation thereof, he demanded such from his wise men. His own professional wise men having failed him in the crucial hour he sent out an edict that the wise men should be slain. Daniel asked for time, prayed mightily to Jehovah and was rewarded

by having the secret revealed to him. The dream and also the interpretation were given to the king and Daniel was made chief governor of Babylon.

(3) The third test was the result of Nebuchadnezzar's dream of the great tree. As usual the king turned to the wrong source for help. The magicians and soothsayers failed again. Daniel again rises to the occasion, gives the interpretation of the great tree in the midst of the earth, exhorts the king to break off his sins by righteousness, shew mercy to the poor and thus lengthen his tranquillity. Ample proof is here afforded of the devotion to God, faithfulness to truth and fearlessness in witnessing for Jehovah before the mighty monarch of Babylon. No wonder Daniel was a man greatly beloved by God.

(4) The fourth test was after the ruin and restoration of Nebuchadnezzar. Belshazzar made a great feast and drank wine before thousands of his lords and subjects. In a drunken frenzy he profaned the sacred vessels of Jehovah which brought upon his unholy head the judgments of God. A man's hand wrote over against the candlestick upon the plaster of the wall of the palace, the kings countenance was changed and conscience stricken and trembling from head to heel the terrified trifler cried aloud for his professional wiseacres, offering scarlet clothes, gold chains, and high honors to anyone who shall read the writing. When all else had failed God's holy Daniel was brought in before the king. Daniel preached a master message to a great audience which included a great king and at least a thousand of his leading lords and ladies. Daniel thunders out the charge against the profane Belshazzar accusing him of pride, sin against light, and profanity, and forthwith pronounces his doom. In that night Belshazzar was slain.

(5) Daniel's fifth test was during the reign of Darius the Median. Darius promoted Daniel making him chief executive, chancellor and premier of the great empire of the Medes and Persians. The loftiest mountains have the most storms to

endure, the tree that bears the best fruit is always the most shaken and stoned, and hence Daniel was headed for greater storms and tempests.

Having been preferred above all the presidents and princes, and having proved himself honorable and trustworthy, the king proposed to set him over the whole realm. This was too much for the jealous office seekers and holders. A storm of hurricane proportions began to brew. Daniel was only a youth compared to some of them. He was also a foreigner, and that of course was an unpardonable sin to many narrow minded professional patriots. Then again he was just a slave and really should be shining the shoes of the sovereign and his satraps. Again, he was with the Babylonians and therefore would never be a loyal Persian. Last, but not least he could not possibly pray three times a day without neglecting his departmental duties. These and other reasons could easily be hashed up against him, but perhaps they could all be answered and thus Daniel would win the day. After carefully weighing all the facts and evidence they came to the conclusion that the only possible way to trap Daniel and find occasion against him would be through his religious convictions. They fooled the king into signing a decree prohibiting all prayer to any person except Darius. The penalty for a first offence was the den of lions. Daniel knew the writing was signed. Returning to his private residence he prayed and praised just as he had previously done. Daniel and Darius were trapped. Daniel unflinchingly and unhesitatingly chose death rather than compromise with his conscience or conduct. The God of Daniel again proved Himself as the one able to deliver. The lions were given the lock-jaw because Daniel believed in God. Daniel's triumph was complete. Daniel honored God and God honored Daniel.

II. The Visions of Nebuchadnezzar

(1) The Great Image.

Nebuchadnezzar dreamed that he saw a great image with its head of gold, its breast and arms of silver, abdomen of brass, legs of iron and feet part iron and part clay. A stone cut out without hands crashed into the image and smashed it to pieces. The smiting stone became a great mountain and filled the earth. The great-terrible-man-image-dream was interpreted by Daniel. The head of gold was Babylon and Nebuchadnezzar, the breast and arms of silver was the Medo Persian Empire under Cyrus and Darius, the abdomen of brass was the Grecian Empire under Alexander the Great, the legs of iron set forth the Roman Empire while the feet represent the present mixture of autocracy and democracy. The stone represents Christ in superhuman, supernatural, smiting power, smashing to smithereens the empires of man and setting up his own glorious millennial kingdom.

(2) The tree in the midst of the earth.

Nebuchadnezzar was at rest in his house, prosperous, pompous and proud in his palace. He dreamed a dream which made him afraid. He saw a great, growing, spreading, fruitful tree in the midst of the earth. Its leaves were beautiful and its fruit was plentiful. It provided shelter for beasts and fowls and was world famous. Suddenly an ax is lifted and the tree is felled to the ground and in the crash and collapse, the King awakens out of his dream. The interpretation is revealed to Daniel. The tree was a symbol of Nebuchadnezzar as king of Babylon, world famous ruler of a world wide empire. The leaves were the people, the fruit were his children, beautiful and prosperous. The hewing down of the tree and the ruin of its fruit was the outcome of the direct decision of watching spirit-angelic-agencies. The sin of Nebuchadnezzar was to be punished by the dissolution and destruction of the Empire and by the temporary insanity of the King. Imagining himself an animal, Nebuchadnezzar was to live under the open canopy of heaven, eat grass instead of grouse and chaff instead of chicken until he learned that Jehovah God ruled in the kingdom of men, and that those who walk in pride He is able to abase. What the goodness and grace of God had failed to accomplish an insane asylum out of doors was to accomplish. For seven years Nebuchadnezzar was to be insane until he knew that God was God and man was only man. Twelve months grace was given wherein the king might find time to repent, but man is slow to learn. While the proud monarch with boastful lips was congratulating himself upon his self made greatness and glory, the judgments of God fell. Driven from men, he became the companion of senseless unclean beasts till his hairs were grown like eagles' feathers and his nails like birds' claws. It does not pay to go against God.

III. The three Hebrews cast into a fiery furnace

Nebuchadnezzar's dream of a great terrible-man-image had evidently left an indelible impression on the mind of the mighty Monarch. He conceived the idea of a colossal image of gold, ordered its manufacture and creation and then issued a proclamation that it should be worshipped. It was one more satanic attempt to damn the race wholesale. Three Holy Hebrews refused to forsake the God of the Bible and His worship, either to keep their jobs, homes or heads. The mad monarch ordered the furnace heated to white heat, and the helpless holy Hebrews were flung into the fiery flames. They fell down bound into the midst of the merciless flames. God, the God of the Hebrews, the God of the Bible, the God of Abraham, Isaac, Jacob, Moses, Elijah and Elisha, stepped into the fiery furnace with His faithful followers and fully delivered them so that the fire had no power. Not even a hair of their head was singed nor the smell of fire passed upon them. Truly, there is no other God that can deliver after this sort.

There is history, profit and prophecy in this account. In a day that is yet to dawn another boastful ruler will make another great image and all the world ordered to bow before it and woe to the man or woman, who like the three Hebrews will dare to brook the wrath of that coming one. Nebuchadnezzar was a type of the coming Anti-Christ. The image will not only be set up, but made to talk and the Great Tribulation furnace heated seven times more than has ever been experienced by mortal man. The faithful remnant of the closing days of the great tribulation will be taken through it and saved out of it. The God of Shadrach, Meshach and Abednego is to deliver his holy people in the latter days of the indignation. Truly there is no other God that can deliver after this sort.

IV. Belshazzar's great feast

Refusing to profit by the example of Nebuchadnezzar's insanity and wrapped in false security, Belshazzar made a great feast. A thousand of his lords were with him, and while in a drunken frenzy he ordered the vessels that were taken out of the temple of God filled with unholy wine. Not content with this desecration of sacred things they praised the gods of Babylon and thus insulted the God of the Hebrews. A man's hand wrote upon the plaster of the wall and the king saw the hand that wrote. The king's countenance was changed, his thoughts troubled him, the joints of his loins were loosed, his knees smote and terror stricken, he called for help. Belshazzar's sin had reached such a height, there was no remedy. No word of exhortation such as that given to Nebuchadnezzar was uttered. No call to repentance was sounded and no word of hope was given. Belshazzar had crossed the line between God's mercy and his wrath, his doom was at hand and that night the king of the Chaldeans was slain.

V. Daniel's Visions

(1) The Vision of the four great beasts.

Daniel saw the rise and fall of the only four world empires which have ever swayed a sceptre over the earth. (1) Babylon (2) Persia (3) Greece (4) Rome. He also saw the future Anti-Christ who is to make war with the saints and spread desolation over the earth. He saw the Anti-Christ in all his fury prevail against the saints until Christ their king appear in glory to deliver them.

(2) Vision of the Ram and he Goat.

Daniel gives a prophetic foreview of the whole future history of the Medo-Persian kingdom, the rise and fall of Alexander the Great, and the fierce, murderous, Jew hating Antiochus Epiphanes. Daniel was so affected by this divine revelation that he fainted and for a few days was unable to attend to his state duties. God knows the end from the beginning. The future is as clear to God as the histories of the past.

(3) The closing vision vouchsafed to Daniel concerns the doings of kings and nations from the days of Cyrus to the opening of the New Testament Scriptures. The leagues and conflicts between the kings north and south of Palestine are minutely foretold and history has verified the prophecy. The final revelation deals with the apocalypse of the Anti-Christ. He shall be a real person, shall do according to his own will, exalt himself, and declare himself to be God. He shall be a boastful blasphemer, an apostate Jew, defiant of the God of his fathers. He shall be an avowed enemy of Christ, an outstanding militarist and dictator (Read v. 36-39). He shall be a Napoleon, Nero, Mussolini, Pope Lenin, and Hitler all in one.

THE PERSONAL HISTORY OF DANIEL

The book of Daniel naturally falls into two parts. The first six chapters are historic and the last six are prophetic. All history is simply prophecy fulfilled and all prophecy is simply history pre-written. The book of Daniel is a "lamp shining in a dark place." It sets forth in unmistakable terms the presence and power of Jehovah God in the government of the world to the end of time. It reveals God as moving steadily forward to the fulfillment of all His gracious and glorious plans and purposes despite the opposition of the world, the flesh and the devil.

1

THE PERSONAL HISTORY OF DANIEL

Nebuchadnezzar

The word Nebuchadnezzar means "Nebo protects" or "The protection of Nebo" or "Prince of Nebo."

Nebo was the chief god of many heathen worshippers including the king of Babylon. Bel and Nebo were his chief gods. NEBO was the supposed "prince of the gods" and a god of fire. The word Nebuchadnezzar "prince and lord of Nebo" is thus pregnant with meaning. He was named in honor of the heathen god NEBO. *Nebuchadnezzar, king of Babylon*—was God's chosen servant to punish Israel for her sins (Jeremiah 27:6). Jerusalem had been unconquerable because it was the city and the glory of Jehovah. All enemies had been held in check by the power of Israel's God, but when the cup of Jerusalem's iniquity was full, Nebuchadnezzar was chosen by God to become the first world ruler of Gentile times. Both Nebuchadnezzar and Cyrus were God's servants sent to punish Israel because of their sins. The Lord gave Jehoiakim into his hand. The wages of sin is bondage and death. Over a hundred years previous to its fall, the prophet Isaiah had foretold the coming of the Babylonians to spoil Jerusalem (Isa. 38:4-7). Jehoiakim was carried into captivity by the act of Jehovah God. Nebuchadnezzar was God's instrument, God's rod, God's whip to chastise the apostate prince and people. Three times Nebuchadnezzar attacked Jerusalem (1) 606 B.C. (2) 598 B.C. (3) 587 B.C. In the first onslaught he carried off Daniel and his three companions. In the second attack he carried off Ezekiel and in the third and devastating holocaust he burned the city and temple.

Jehoiakim

The word Jehoiakim means "The Lord will set up," "The Lord will establish." There are sermons in Bible names.

The Cross and the Crown may be traced through the scriptures from Genesis to Malachi and from Matthew to Revelation. There is a red line of blood running from Eden in Genesis to the Lamb as it had been slain, of Revelation. Side by side with this red line of redeeming blood is a purple line of royalty beginning with the first Adam in Genesis and concluding with the last Adam (Christ of Revelation 21 and 22.)

This crimson stream (Cross) together with the purple stream (crown) occupies the bulk of Biblical history and prophecy.

The name Jehoiakim assures us that God will set up and establish His Kingdom. The words "Thy kingdom come" are more than pious words. They are to be literally fulfilled in a day which is yet to dawn.

The Land of Shinar:

"And the beginning of his kingdom was Babel [Babylon] ... in the land of Shinar" (Gen. 10:10). (See also Gen. 11:2, Isa. 11:11). Amraphel was king of Shinar (Babylon) during the days of Abraham (Gen. 14:1). The land of Shinar thus stands for Babylon.

The Treasure House:

All spoils of war were taken into the treasure house. Nebuchadnezzar was an idolater and the treasure house of his god was a place appropriated for the reception of war trophies which were thus consecrated to the deity to which the temple belonged.

Of the King's Seed:

Daniel was evidently of the seed royal. Descended from royalty he was now a slave. Behold what sin hath wrought. Sin means slavery.

The learning of the Chaldeans:

Babylon was the capital of ancient learning. "Here were the great libraries of the Semitic race. Here were the scholars who copied so painstakingly every little omen or legend that had come down to them out of the hoary past. Here were the men who had calculated eclipses, watched the moon's changes, and looked nightly from observatories upon the stately march of constellations over the sky."

Now among these were Daniel

Daniel and his companions were taken captive in the summer of B.C. 606.

Daniel suffered because of the sins of others. His fathers had sinned and instead of being a prince he was now a slave. Sin makes paupers out of princes whereas grace and holiness makes princes out of paupers. Through all the trying and changing scenes of his everyday life, however, Daniel kept his conscience clear and clean. His all was consecrated to God and God's will.

Daniel the prophet, like his fellow prisoner-prophet Ezekiel, was a Jewish exile in Babylon. His rank and comeliness commended him to the prince of the eunuchs, and he was specially trained for service in the palace of the king. In the polluted atmosphere of the oriental court, Daniel lived a life of exemplary piety and purity. God honored him by bringing him into favor and tender love with those in authority over him. God honored him still more by making him the prophet of the "times of the Gentiles" not only dealing with the awful apostasy of God's people Israel, but prophesying in clear terms the rise and fall of Gentile kingdoms, the future apocalypse of "the man of sin," the great tribulation, the return of the Messiah, the resurrections, and judgments. The visions and prophecies of Daniel sweep the whole course of Gentile world rule until the Messiah ends it all by one sudden crushing blow after which He sets up his own mighty and glorious millennial kingdom.

Daniel

The word Daniel means "The judge of God" or "God is my judge." We may learn two lessons from his name.

(1) Daniel was God's REPRESENTATIVE on earth. He was God's mouthpiece and representative in the midst of heathendom. He was one of God's representative saints.

(2) It is an encouragement to know that MAN is not our judge. "God is my judge." The final word is not with man but with God.

According to Daniel 1:3 and 1 Chron. 3:1 it is more than likely that Daniel was of royal blood and therefore a type of Christ. His name was changed to Belteshazzar ("Prince of Bel"). The change of name from "Judge of God" to "Prince of Bel" did not however, change either his heart or his life.

Hananiah, Mishael and Azariah:

The word Daniel means "God is my judge," Hananiah means "Beloved of Jehovah," Mishael means "Who is like God," and Azariah means "Jehovah is my help." Let us remember these cheering lessons. (1) God is my judge (not man.) (2) The grace of God is more than sufficient for every need and in any or every emergency. (3) Holiness is Godlikeness or godliness. (4) Help is nigh when God is nigh. In times of testing and trial, in days of darkness and distress, sorrow or sickness, God is a very present help. There are sermons in each of these names.

He gave unto Daniel the name of Belteshazzar

Daniel means "God is my Judge;" Hananiah means "Beloved of the Lord," Mishael means "Godlike" or "who is like God." Azariah means "The Lord is my help." These meaningful Hebrew names were changed to Belteshazzar (prince of Bel) Shadrach (the sun god) Meshach (like Shack) Abednego (servant of Nego.) Nebuchadnezzar attempted to blot out the name and memory of the Jehovah of hosts and God of the Hebrews.

Belteshazzar:

The name Belteshazzar was given to Daniel in honor of Bel the god of Nebuchadnezzar. Nebuchadnezzar thus made a desperate but vain attempt to obliterate the name of Jehovah and all remembrance of Him.

Not once does God or the Holy Spirit, the angels, or the prophet himself use the word Belteshazzar. The word itself was intended to be a flattering title, for it means "The prince of Bel." Satan's idea was to get rid of the God of Abraham, Isaac; Jacob and Israel!

1. Daniel "God is my judge" was changed to Belteshazzar "Prince of Bel."
2. Hananiah "Jehovah favors" was changed to Shadrach "Inspired or illumined by the Sun-god."
3. Mishael "Who is like God or Godlike" was changed to Meshach "Who is like Shak" one of the Babylonian idols.
4. Azariah "Jehovah helps" was changed to Abednego "Servant of Nego."

Thus honor was paid to four of the gods of Babylon and a subtle satanic attempt was made to get rid of the God of the Hebrews. The chief god was Bel and hence "Belteshazzar." Then came the "Sun-god" Shadrach, the "Earth-god" Meshach and the "Fire-god, Abednego.

But Daniel purposed in his heart

Daniel could not avoid being captured by the Chaldean army, he could not prevent the Gentile king changing his name, he could neither hinder his own confinement, nor the confinement of his companions in the court of the Chaldeans, he could not prevent the King from dictating certain foods and drink—BUT, he could refuse to change his life and he could refuse to eat THE FORBIDDEN FOOD. Daniel determined to be true to God whatever the cost or consequences. Where Adam and Eve failed, Daniel, under Divine grace, succeeded.

Daniel purposed . . . that he would not:

There are certain things which a child of God can not and will not do.
(1) He will not act contrary to God's will as revealed in His Word.
(2) He will not go contrary to His God.
(3) He will not violate his own enlightened conscience. "Daniel would not."

He would not defile himself

Had Daniel compromised with the Word of God, trifled with his convictions and tinkered with his conscience, either for personal safety or for political preferment, pomp or power he never could have been the channel through whom God poured forth his truth to kings and kingdoms both past and present. God was preparing this youth for future revelations of his word and will.

Not only were pork, bacon and wine forbidden in the Deuteronomic law but the food placed before Daniel and his three Hebrew friends may have been sacrificed to idols and hence a second good reason why Daniel purposed in his heart that he would not defile himself.

"Be not conformed" to Babylon, Chicago, Paris, New York, or Kansas City. Be transformed by the renewing of your mind. To be conformed means to run parallel with. To be transformed means to go across. Daniel refused to run parallel with Babylon. *Are we running parallel with or across?* How about the card table? theatre? talkies? the dance? the cigarette? wine glass? dress? worldly sports? divorce? birth control? Parallel with or across? which? Conformed or transformed? which? Daniel would not defile himself. How about you?

Whether defilement to which allusion is here made arose (1) from certain food being prohibited by the law of Moses as unclean or (2) because of the custom of offering food to idols or (3) food which had been dedicated to an idol (See 1 Cor.

8:10) Daniel would not defile himself. Do not defile yourself. Do not defile your MIND, your EYES, your BODY, your LIPS, your TONGUE, your FINGERS, your SOUL, *do not defile yourself.*

Daniel purposed . . . requested:

Daniel's conduct in our day would be dubbed as "narrow-mindedness and puritanical bigotry." Daniel however was more concerned about the smile of God than the handclaps of the giddy and godless crowd. Daniel kept a conscience void of offence toward God and man and God honored his holy servant.

Therefore he requested:

The humble attitude and petition of Daniel was the direct consequence of a high purpose not to defile himself. We have (1) High Purpose as THE ROOT "Daniel purposed in his heart" (2) Holy Practice as THE FRUIT "He would not," (3) Happy Privilege "Therefore he requested."

That he might not defile himself:

Daniel purposed in his heart that he would not and then made a courteous request that he might not defile himself. Temptations are to be fairly met and firmly resisted. Temptations are to be resisted in a right and proper way. The heart must be holy, the will must be set, the life must be winning, the protest must be courteously borne, and then the results awaited with faith and patience.

Daniel first purposed, and then requested. He was wise. He did not purpose and then rudely refuse. He purposed, for that was right and then he requested for that was the part of wisdom. As a rule we are persecuted more for our foolishness, rashness, stubbornness, and rudeness rather than for righteousness sake.

Melzar:

Melzar was the STEWARD or college DEAN under Ashpenaz the chief of the eunuchs.

Pulse to eat

Pulse or cereal, as we would express it, was the food of the laboring classes. The "pulse" of verses 12 and 16 included barley, wheat, rye and probably peas and beans.

Their countenance appeared fairer and fatter

Godliness is profitable. Profitable for time and eternity. Profitable for body, mind and soul. Faithfulness to God and consecration to his will always react on the face of the faithful.

A little with God is better than much without God. The presence and blessing of God are more important than fatted hogs and boiled beans.

NEBUCHADNEZZAR'S DREAM
WORLD HISTORY FORETOLD

Statesmen would do well to study and search the sacred scriptures. Important decisions could then be made in direct harmony with the Divine decrees. Daniel wrote the history of the Gentile nations as accurately as a historian could describe it today. He foresaw the end of the great Babylonian empire, the rise and fall of the Medo-Persian empire, the coming and crashing of all Grecian greatness as well as the rise and ruin of the Empire of Rome. The Bible holds the key to the present world situation.

NEBUCHADNEZZAR'S DREAM

Nebuchadnezzar dreamed dreams

God used an ass to rebuke the madness of the lucre loving prophet, Balaam. He commissioned a raven to carry fresh meat to the hungry prophet Elijah. He ordained a rooster to reprove the backslidings of an apostle Peter. He stretched a roaring lion across the path of a Timnath descending Samson. He warned a sinning Saul through the bleating of an innocent sheep and he honored a heathen king with one of the most far reaching visions ever vouchsafed to mortal man. God is always doing the unusual.

His spirit was troubled

The dream had made a lasting impression upon the mind of Nebuchadnezzar. Conscience, which makes cowards of all wrong doers, was troubling the wicked monarch. His mind was distressed, his spirit was troubled.

The dream of Nebuchadnezzar must have carried with it an incontestable evidence of its divine origin and prophetic importance. Nebuchadnezzar was a troubler of God's people, but God was the troubler of Nebuchadnezzar. We know not the restlessness and unease of many who live in great pomp and put on a big, boastful outside show. We look into their houses and watch their extravagant ways and are tempted to envy, but could we look into their hearts we should pity rather than envy them.

I have dreamed a dream

At sundry times and in divers manners God has revealed his righteous will to men. Pharaoh's dream of the fat and lean kine was skilfully interpreted by Joseph. Jacob's dream of a ladder was a foreshadowing of Christ who was to bridge the gulf between a holy God and sinful men. God leads, guides and directs by his providences, by dreams, by His Spirit and by His word.

Syriac

Daniel 2:3 to 6:28 inclusive is written in the Aramaic or Syriac language. The remaining portions of the Book of Daniel was written in Hebrew. That which was of supreme interest to the Gentiles was written in their own language. It seems as if God would say to the Gentile world, Read here what shall become of your pomp, pride, and power. Learn here the end of your boasted civilization and genius.

Your houses shall be a dunghill

The king's answer displays the arrogance, violence and impetuosity of his character. It also serves to illustrate the evil tendency and fatal effect of arbitrary power placed into the hands of puny man. The king's apparent anxiety to understand the dream might have been produced by his fear of some sudden revolution in his empire. Whatever was in his mind he was determined to brook no delay in executing his barbarous decree.

Ye shall be cut in pieces

This passage strikingly illustrates the character of ancient monarchs. Nothing can exceed the ferocity, arrogance, wickedness, and arbitrary violence of these reckless rulers. Pride and passion seemed to prevail while human life was held horribly cheap.

They were to be dismembered, limb from limb and thus their condemnation not only included death but also involved the deprivation of the rights of a proper burial.

A dunghill:

The greatest disgrace was thus to be inflicted on the memory of the condemned. Their punishment was therefore to be three-fold (1) death, (2) dismemberment, (3) disgrace.

Ye would gain the time

The king evidently thought that they were trifling either to give them time to invent something or make an escape after having packed up their belongings.

There is not a man upon the earth that can shew the king's matter

This sets forth the impotency of oriental arts and professions. There are some things beyond the reach of all human knowledge or created genius.

Apart from GOD'S REVELATION it is impossible to know GOD'S WILL. Daniel in the Old Testament received the interpretation from above and Christ became a man from heaven to reveal God's will in the New Testament.

They sought Daniel . . . to be slain

On account of the youth of Daniel and his companions they were left out of the consultative councils. They were deemed unfit for consultation, but not for condemnation. Here is a flagrant example of the injustice of the despotic king and counsellors. Satan was thus making a bold bid for the destruction of Daniel and his holy companions.

He would shew the king the interpretation

With confidence in God and using the language of faith, Daniel wisely answered Arioch. He evidently knew that the same God in whom he trusted had given Joseph wisdom while in Egypt and here revealed the fact that the same God lived in his own dark days.

Mercies from the God of heaven

All answered prayer is a mercy from the God of heaven. We receive answers to prayer not because of our merits or rights, but because of the mercies of the God of heaven. We may receive nothing by way of recompense for our goodness or holiness, but all as the gift of God's goodness and grace.

Then was the secret revealed

The test was passed, the battle was won, the victory was complete. An all night of prayer solved the pressing problem. The matter was spread before the God of heaven and then was the secret revealed. More secrets would be revealed if there were more all-night prayer meetings among God's holy people. MORE PRAYER would bring MORE SECRETS and all would end in MORE PRAISE.

Then Daniel blessed . . . God

After prayer is answered, praise is in order. Daniel did not excitedly run off into the presence of the king of Babylon. He first of all had a shouting spell before Jehovah and then went in unto Arioch.

Wisdom and might are his

This is one of the great truths emphasized and illustrated in the book of Daniel. This book with its mystic messages, its strange symbols, its days and dates, its beasts and birds and its times and half times sets forth in no uncertain terms that God is sovereign Lord and supreme ruler of all. WISDOM is not only knowing but knowing HOW, WHEN, WHERE, and WHY. The word *Might* speaks of ability to execute, rule or overrule according as wisdom directs.

God knows all things and can do all things. Thus is set for both the omniscience (wisdom) and omnipotence (might) of the God of the Bible.

He removeth kings and setteth up kings

God is the ruling and overruling one, setting up and removing kings as His wisdom directs and dictates. God is the overruling God, in wisdom knowing and in might working, setting up and casting down, permitting evil to work out its own ultimate destruction and preserving good to its full development and final triumph.

I thank thee

"Then was the secret revealed unto Daniel in a night vision. Then Daniel blessed the God of heaven. Daniel answered and said, Blessed be the name of God for ever and ever: for wisdom and might are his: And he changeth the times and the seasons; he removeth kings, and setteth up kings: he giveth wisdom unto the wise, and knowledge to them that know understanding: He revealeth the deep and secret things; he knoweth what is in the darkness, and the light dwelleth with him. *I thank thee,* and praise thee, O thou God of my fathers, who hast given me wisdom and might, and hast made known unto me now what we desired of thee; for thou hast now made known unto us the king's matter." Here is a classical passage on the great question of thanksgiving. What a text for a thanksgiving day sermon.

I have found a man

How vain is man! In the ages past Satan said "I will ascend—I will exalt myself." Pharaoh also said "I will pursue, I will overtake." Arioch follows with his false "I have found a man" as if the discovery of Daniel and Daniel's abilities was owing purely to his own great diligence and sagacity.

I have found a man

A man. I have found a man. "Gird up now thy loins like a man," God called to the fainting Job. Here is the need of the hour. MEN. Men, not methods. Men, not machinery. Men, not rules and regulations. Men, not plans and programs but MEN. Men like Daniel. "I have found a man."

The latter days

This expression refers to the times of the Messiah. It takes in all time from the birth of Christ to his coming and kingdom. The latter days refer to the birth, ministry and millennial reign of Christ as Messiah. The crown rather than the cross is in view in the Old Testament.

That thou mightest know

God does not will that any man should remain in ignorance. Daniel's interpretation of Nebuchadnezzar's dream is the most amazing panorama of world history ever unveiled to the mind of man by the mighty creator.

A great image

A comprehensive outline of the prophetic future may be found in the book of ISAIAH. Interesting and instructive details as to the closing days of this age are given in the book of Zechariah. Ezekiel foretells the religious and civil state of Israel during the millennium. The rise, growth, course, decay and doom of the Gentile powers are minutely unfolded in the prophecies of Daniel.

This image gives the outward imposing greatness and magnificence of the Gentile world-powers. The vision of Daniel and the beasts reveal the inward bestial condition of all world dominion.

Head of Gold:

This head of gold was Babylon with Nebuchadnezzar as its first God ordained ruler. Babylon was called THE GOLDEN CITY (Isaiah 14:4; Jer. 51:7; Rev. 18:16). Babylon was by far the greatest and richest city of the world.

Romans: 15:4 "For whatsoever things were written aforetime were written for our learning, that we through patience and comfort of the scriptures might have hope."

Had Christ taken the earth kingdom at His first coming, He would have taken them from Satan's hands (Matt. 4:1-10). The present kingdoms and their passing glories belong to Satan and when he and they have filled up the measure of iniquity Christ shall descend and by force of His own Omnipotent arm He shall set up and establish His own universal and unending kingdom.

From Gold to Clay and from Stone to Mountain—gives the whole history of the world from the days of Nebuchadnezzar to the millennial kingdom of Christ.

Feet ... part clay

The whole stately looking colossus of man stands on weak feet. ALL man's glory is supported only by mud! The world powers contain in themselves the elements of deterioration, devolution, decay, destruction and death. They stand on a foundation of clay. The mighty Metallic image lessens in specific gravity as it goes downward from the head of gold to the feet which are part clay.

The course, character and coming crisis of Gentile dominion and man's day is thus clearly declared. Its COURSE is downward, from gold to clay. ITS CHARACTER is bestial and senseless, from a man as seen by Nebuchadnezzar to a beast as seen by Daniel. ITS COMING CRISIS is yet future when Christ the Smiting Stone descends and pulverizes it to powder. That this smashing of the Gentile world powers by the Smiting Stone cannot refer to Christ at His first advent may clearly be seen by remembering that the fourth kingdom of the LEGS OF IRON was then in existence whereas The Stone falls upon the feet ... part iron and part clay.

EXCELLENT and TERRIBLE

Excellent, in that it attracts. The bright lights, entrancing music, fashionable parties and feasts, scientific accomplishments, education, sports, bank accounts, stocks and bonds, etc.

Terrible because of that which repels. Lust, murder, robbery, adultery, strife, war and hell, etc.

Excellent and terrible

Here is a two word complete description of the kingdoms of the world. *Excellent* and *terrible,* characterize the history of all Gentile powers from the days of Nebuchadnezzar to the coming of Christ with His Saints. There is that which attracts and also that which repels. There is that which is excellent but side by side with the excellent there is that which is terrible. These features are to characterize this age and continue until Christ sets up His millennium.

A stone . . . upon his feet

Christ is the stone (Isa. 8:14; Psa. 118:22; Acts 4:11). The Stone smites the image, not in the head (Babylonian times) nor in the body (Persian and Grecian times) nor in the legs (Roman times in which Christ was born as a babe) but on the feet and toes (yet future). Not when Babylon was broken, nor when Persia perished, nor when Greece was given to its four generals, nor at the birth, death or resurrection of our blessed Lord, nor on the day of Pentecost, nor at the Reformation, did this mighty colossus crash. It still exists. The ten toes and ten horns are yet to come and anyone today with eyes to see and ears to hear must be aware of the fact that the tribulation comes on apace. The Anti-Christ with the mark of the Beast seems just around the corner. Then the coming of Christ to reign and the imposing Colossus shall crash.

Men . . . beast . . . fowls

This was the dominion originally given to man and which he forfeited by sin (Gen. 1:28 and 2:19-20). The same was given to Noah after the flood and later delegated to the Gentiles under Nebuchadnezzar. Instead of using all good things for the glory of God and the good of mankind they abuse the trust for self. Not until the return of Christ shall the lost inheritance be fully restored.

Part of iron and part of clay

Deterioration, decay and devolution mark the course of Gentile dominion. It begins with gold and ends with mud. Gold is more precious than silver; silver than brass; brass than iron; iron than clay. The difference between shining gold and slimy clay is immense. This prophecy strikes the death blow to the modern evolutionary hypothesis. The evolutionists and the modernists have this image down side up. They have stood Nebuchadnezzar's image on its head. Moreover, the first power (Babylon) was a unit, the second (Medes and Persians) dual; the third (Greece) became quadruple; the fourth (Rome) in its final form is to be decimal-ten toes in the image and ten horns in the beast. Thus there is deterioration by admixture and also by division. Constitutional unity declines until it fades out into democratic license, communistic killings and socialistic suicide. IRON denotes the monarchistic, imperialistic, unyielding element while clay presents the plastic and popular element *and the two cannot blend*.

The feet and toes, part of potter's clay

The tremendous weight of imperial government is here seen to be resting on a base which is composed in part of potter's clay. Here is strikingly set forth the present uncertain, unstable, insecure and already tottering governments of earth with all their boasted scientific inventions and civilization. The whole ponderous mass is seen to be standing on a foundation part of potter's clay. The last great war almost spelled the collapse of our vaunted twentieth century culture and civilization. The next war will find the whole world utterly bankrupt and its civilization doomed. The whole superstructure is here seen to be resting on a weak foundation, part of potter's clay. It is with holy awe that we perceive the soon termination of the times of the Gentiles and the arrival in power and glory of God's King from heaven.

The distance between gold and mud is immense and yet in such terms the divine penman sets forth the deterioration and devolution of the kingdoms and nations of the earth. Modern unbelief with its evolutionary hypothesis has the metallic man standing on his head.

The feet and toes

Babylon (B.C. 606-538) Medo-Persia (B.C. 538-331) Greece (B.C. 331-168) Rome (B.C. 168-A.D. 476). The feet of iron (strength-monarchy) and clay (weakness-democracy-socialism and anarchy) (A.D. 476 ——?)

The years given for Babylon, Medo-Persia, Greece, and Rome severally are not intended to cover the entire history of

NEBUCHADNEZZAR'S DREAM / 43

these nations, but only the period during which each of these great powers exercised world dominance. The long dash after A.D. 476 signifies that we are still in the divided state of the Roman Empire, which division is to continue until Christ returns.

Part of potter's clay

Daniel foresees the democracies of our own Laodicean age —foretells the disintegration and disruption resulting therefrom.

"Look for the waymarks as you journey on,
  Look for the waymarks, passing one by one;
Down through the ages, past the kingdoms four—
  Where are we standing? Look the waymarks o'er.
"Down in the feet of iron and of clay
  Weak and divided, soon to pass away;
What will the next great, glorious drama be?
  Christ and His coming, and eternity."

Mixed with miry clay

The prophecies of Daniel reveal the fact that constitutional unity in government was to decline until it finally fades out into democratic license and communistic anarchy. The decline from gold to clay gives the death blow to Evolution unless the metallic man is made to stand upon his head. IRON denotes the strength of imperialism and the unyielding element in monarchies whereas CLAY sets forth the plastic and popular elements of democracy. The two cannot blend.

They shall not cleave one to another

Here is a plain prophecy of the breaking up of world governments and world civilization. The world economic and monetary conference held in London in 1933 with SIXTY-SIX nations in solemn assembly sat in the world famous city of London. The eyes of the world were focussed on London. Hopes were high, but all hope centered in man is vain. The conference collapsed. "They shall not cleave one to another."

One Lord, one faith, one baptism, one God and one King—CHRIST—is God's program for the race. Here is the most down-to-date exhibition and illustration of this remarkable prophetic passage.

In the days of these kings

The time of the destruction of the present world order is clearly revealed. "It is in the days of these kings." After the rapture of the Church, after the apocalypse of the Anti-Christ, and while the earth is ruled by ten dictators with Anti-Christ at the head, the smiting stone (Christ) will descend and with one supernatural, smashing stroke destroy all Gentile dominion and the kingdoms of this world shall become the kingdoms of our Lord and of His Christ. All other kingdoms shall be broken in pieces and consumed by the Smiting Stone and then shall the God of heaven set up a kingdom which shall never be destroyed.

Christ's kingdom shall know no decay, and shall never be in danger of revolution. It shall never be destroyed. Christ shall be a King unconquerable and unconquered—a monarch without a successor.

In the days of these kings:

Here is a definite time set for the Stone to do its smiting work. THE TEN KINGS which arise after the rapture of the Saints will rule over that part of the world which was once governed by the Old Roman Empire. Five of those kings will rule over the Eastern Division and five over the Western Division of the now divided and disrupted Roman Empire. Ten kings will be ruling over the divided Roman Empire just before the apocalypse of the Anti-Christ and three years and a half after the Anti-Christ has begun his devilish, wicked work, Christ, the Smiting Stone shall descend, and sweep the whole sinful business from the face of the earth. Seizing the reigns of government in his own Sovereign hands Christ shall fill the earth with His own presence, power and glory, and the oft repeated prayer, "Thy Kingdom Come" shall at last be answered for Christ shall be Supreme.

The next event for which all creation waits is the Return of Christ. At His Second advent the sleeping saints shall awake and the living saints shall be raptured and all together shall be caught up to meet the Lord in the air. Hell shall be let loose on the earth. Ten kings, rulers, dictators shall arise and rule the earth. During the dictatorship of the ten kings the Anti-Christ shall appear. The incarnation of wilfulness and wickedness, the Anti-Christ shall soon dominate the world and after seven years of hell on earth the Smiting Stone shall descend, and destroy the world empires of man and the Stone having done its Smiting work shall roll on until He fills the earth. "Even so, Come, Lord Jesus!"

The stone:

The smiting stone falls in a destroying judgment on the feet part iron and clay, pulverizing it to powder. This is just the opposite of a so called gradual evangelization and conversion of the world by the gospel, or the Church. The Church is to be subject to the powers and hence the destroying judgments cannot be dealt by Christians. The Stone is Christ Himself and the judgment awaits His return.

The stone was cut out without hands

A NEW MOVEMENT FROM WITHOUT changes the whole course of history! Man had nothing to do with it. It was not of the earth. It was A STONE. It was a stone cut out without hands. It was a supernatural, smiting, smashing, destroying, demolishing stone, and its descent changes the whole course of human history.

Again, the stone does not crowd out the Colossus, it does not diffuse a transforming influence over it, it does not change nor regenerate the image making it a devout God-fearing worshipper. The stone smites, smashes, crushes, destroys and demolishes the metallic image and demolition is not conversion nor is smiting and smashing, salvation. The action of the stone is a judgment action, not of grace; it ruins, rather than regenerates. The times of the Gentiles end in wrath and ruin, not in repentance and regeneration. The Stone (Christ) does not fill the earth until after the crash of the Gentile Colossus.

Seven times in the sacred scriptures our Lord is called a stone. It is the symbol of STRENGTH, DURABILITY, and FIRMNESS. Man may make bricks, but he cannot make a stone! Christ is the Stone (Acts 4:10-11). Christ came in the form of a servant and thus became a stone of stumbling to the nation of Israel. Israel fell on this stone and was broken (Matt. 21:44). Christ is the Rock upon which the Church is built and other foundation must no man lay. Christ is the Stone who is to fall on the stately Colossus of man and grind it to powder (Matt. 21:44; Dan. 2:34-35). Christ is the Stone who shall descend and fill the earth.

Nothing was left but *the stone*. The image was pounded into powder. It was smashed and swept from the earth. The Stone rolled on and on until it filled the earth.

One of the dominant notes of modernists, evolutionists and post-millennialists is that man will end war and that man will bring in the millennium. Since the granting of the franchise to women, many women politicians and would be prophets have affirmed that women and mothers shall end war and bring in the millennium. May we at once go on record as saying that it is not the business of man, either in the world or the church to end war or bring in the millennium. THE BRINGING IN THE MILLENNIUM OF PEACE AND RIGHTEOUSNESS WAITS THE COMING OF THE SMITING STONE. The God of heaven and not man is to set up a kingdom which shall never be destroyed. The God of heaven and not the Church is to establish the immovable and imperishable Kingdom of Christ among men.

These world powers were neither transformed, converted nor regenerated. They were pulverized, broken in pieces, the wind carried them away and NO PLACE WAS FOUND FOR

THEM. All world power is idolatrous, self willed, sinful, intolerant, defiant of God, blasphemous, and incurably corrupt. This wicked world has always defied God, dishonored Christ, denied his authority, clubbed its Abels, mocked at its Isaacs, sneered at and stoned its saints, poked fun at its prophets, flung its holy youth into furnaces of fire, dropped its Daniels into divers dens, beheaded its fiery Baptists, persecuted its Peters and Pauls, and slain its saints with the sword. Thank God, that in a day which is soon to dawn the Smiting Stone shall descend, smite the world governments and world empires, smash them in pieces, pulverize them into powder and sweep them from the earth so that no place shall be found for them. May God hasten such a day.

From earliest times God began to send the glad message that sin was not forever to stain the earth. RIGHT, shall not forever be on the scaffold and WRONG shall not forever be on the throne. THE SEED OF THE WOMAN shall yet finally and forever destroy the serpent whose head he wounded on Calvary.

Enoch also prophesied saying "Behold the Lord cometh with ten thousand of his saints."

We await the glad hour when Christ shall finish His ministry of intercession on high and come again in power and glory to usher in the kingdom which shall never pass away. That long expected day we sincerely believe is at hand.

"Upon its feet"

The stone did not fall upon the head, or arms, or legs, but upon the feet.

Not when Babylon fell (HEAD).

Nor when Persia was conquered (ARMS).

Nor when Greece was defeated (BODY).

Nor when Rome was in ruins (LEGS).

But UPON ITS FEET, composed of part iron and part clay.

NOT at the birth of Jesus for then none of the world empires were either smitten or smashed.

NOT at the death of Christ for then HE was smitten, despised and rejected of men.

NOT when the Holy Spirit was poured out on the day of Pentecost for that was during the reign of the LEGS of IRON and they certainly were not destroyed on the day of Pentecost.

NOT when Saul of Tarsus was converted and changed to Paul the missionary for that also was during the sovereignty of THE LEGS OF IRON. They smote the Apostle, took off his head and enabled him to win a martyr's crown. THEN Rome was the smiter and Christ, John, James and Paul were smitten. NOT in past, but in the future when the Anti-Christ shall be at the head of the ten Kingdoms with their ten Kings, shall Christ the Smiting Stone descend and smash the sinful kingdoms of the world and the stone shall roll on until it fills the earth with millennial peace, purity and prosperity. The Stone (Christ) cut out without hands (Divine Christ) shall break in pieces the empires of man.

The stone does not diffuse a transforming, sanctifying influence over the image of gold, silver, brass and iron. Neither does the stone slowly crowd out the Colossus nor change it into a pious peaceful worshipper of God. The stone does not purify the kingdom of the world, IT PULVERIZES THEM and there is quite a difference between purification and pulverization. The Stone does not sanctify the image; it smashes it to smithereens. The Stone does not transform either the monarchies of Babylon, (Head) or Persia, (Arms) or Greece, (Body) or Rome (Legs) or the democracies of Earth, (feet part iron) (strong) (and part clay), (weak). It pulverizes them.

The Stone comes down from the skies and with terrific force crashes into the feet and smashes the image to powder. The Stone neither converts nor consecrates nor cleanses the Colossus. It crashes into it and crushes it to powder. After the Stone has done its work there is not anything left either of Monarchies or Democracies. The Stone fills the earth, thank God! Christ is Conqueror. The Saviour is supreme. Hallelujah!

And worshipped Daniel

Here is the proud and mighty monarch of all the world upon his face before God's holy prophet. Thus is set forth the future humiliation and prostration of all world powers during the coming Millennial Kingdom of Christ.

The stone became a great mountain

The stone came from the mountain originally. It was a part of a magnificent mountain in the beginning and after crashing into the Colossus and smashing it in pieces it ends in becoming a great mountain which fills the earth. The Stone came from heaven in the first place and it ends by bringing heaven to earth.

The stone . . . break in pieces

The stone smites the image, smashing it into powder. By one crushing blow the old kingdoms of man's day and man's sway crash and crumble and the new kingdom of Christ fills the earth. "And I saw heaven opened and behold a white horse; and he that sat upon him was called Faithful and True, and in righteousness he doth judge and make war. His eyes were as a flame of fire and on his head were many crowns; and he had a name written, that no man knew, but he himself. And he was clothed with a vesture dipped in blood: and his name is called The Word of God. And the armies which were in heaven followed him upon white horses, clothed in fine linen, white and clean. And out of his mouth goeth a sharp sword, that with it he should rule them with a rod of iron: and he treadeth the winepress of the fierceness and wrath of Almighty God. And he hath on his vesture and on his thigh a name written, KING OF KINGS, AND LORD OF LORDS" (Rev. 19:11-16).

The day is surely approaching when all Christ's enemies shall become his footstool. It does not pay to go against God. When THE STONE falls it will grind to powder all upon whom it falls.

Victorious over all opposition, Christ shall break in pieces and consume the kingdoms of the earth. The kingdom, the peace and increase of his government shall know no end. After Babylon, Persia, Greece, Rome, Britain and the rest of earth's empires are swept from the groaning earth and their place knows them no more the Kingdom of Christ shall flourish and the followers of Christ shall reign with Him.

Notice:

1. The stone which is to break in pieces was not evolved from the kingdoms that preceded it. It was "CUT OUT OF THE MOUNTAINS."

2. The stone which is to break in pieces and fill the earth was "CUT OUT WITHOUT HANDS." Human effort does not establish the kingdom or convert the nations.

3. The stone "break in pieces." The end of man's rule, man's day, man's way and man's kingdom will come with a crash.

TO ISRAEL Christ was a Stone of Stumbling. Christ warned them that "whatsoever shall fall upon this stone shall be broken" (Matt. 21:44). They fell upon it and as a nation were broken.

TO THE CHURCH, Christ is the living head corner stone and foundation stone (Matt. 16:16-18). The stone which was set at naught by the Jews became the head of the corner, and other foundation can no man lay for there is no other name given among men whereby we must be saved.

TO THE GENTILES, Christ will be the Smiting Stone, who, suddenly appearing shall fall upon them and grind them to powder. The Babel tower of man's civilization shall crash, world dominion by the Gentile nations shall end, and Christ shall fill the earth with righteousness and peace. The Gentile

NEBUCHADNEZZAR'S DREAM / 51

world system is not to be destroyed by the gradual processes of prohibition, disarmament conferences or mass conversions but by a sudden, severe, supernatural blow from a DESCENDING SMITING STONE. The smiting stone becomes a great mountain only after the destruction of the world system of Gentile government and rule.

At His first coming Christ was smitten and crucified. He was put to death by the fourth empire under which he was born as a babe. The destruction of Gentile world rule awaits His second coming in power and great glory. The crushing blow is still suspended. In the meantime Gentile rule follows the course as marked out in this marvelous vision.

That the stone does not refer to the gospel may be clearly seen by the fact that man has nothing to do with either the appearing or the falling of the stone.

Smashing is not salvation. Crushing is NOT conversion. Destroying is NOT delivering nor is Pulverizing the same as purification.

The dream is certain

Nebuchadnezzar was thus exhorted to give earnest heed to the dream and its interpretation. It was not an ordinary dream. It was a perfect revelation of things to come.

An Oblation and sweet odours

Making presents of perfumes was regarded as a mark of reverence and honor. The king intended to do Daniel great honor.

Nebuchadnezzar fell upon his face

The mightiest monarch of all history is here seen prostrated before the devout Daniel. Men must either bow and bend or be broken. Selah!

Daniel sat in the gate of the king

Everything in Chapter 2 is not only historic but is also prophetic. The moral state of Gentile times to the end is therein set forth. Not only so, but chapter 2 is prophetic of the final triumph of God's people. Daniel was made ruler over the whole province of Babylon. His three friends (Jews) were set over the affairs of the province under Daniel, all of which is a foreshadowing of the final triumph of God and God's saints.

The Dream of Nebuchadnezzar (chap. 2)
The Great Image

The key:

"There is a God in heaven that revealeth secrets and maketh known—what shall be in the latter days—what shall come to pass hereafter" (2:28-29).

The Vision	The Interpretation
"Behold a great image" v. 31	A prophetic foreview of all world government.
"This image's head was of fine gold"	Nebuchadnezzar.
"His breast and his arms of silver"	The empire of the Medes and Persians under Cyrus and Darius (two arms)
"His belly and his thighs of brass"	The third world empire of Greece under Alexander the great.
"His legs of iron"	The iron empire of Rome.
"His feet part of iron and part of clay"	The devolution from gold to clay strikes a death blow to evolution. The critics have turned this image upside down.
	The strength of monarchy mixed with the weakness of DEMOCRACY. Our democratic age was thus foreseen by Daniel.
"Thou sawest till that a stone was cut out without hands"	The stone typifies Christ the Conquering King.
"Cut out without hands"	Supernatural, Divine.
	Christ shall destroy all world governments and reign without a rival.
"Which smote the image upon his feet"	Babylon, Persia, Greece and Rome, as world empires were to pass away before the apocalypse of Christ as King.

"Upon his feet"	The glorious appearing of Christ as King of kings was to be during the democratic age. We are now living in the feet era of this great image wherein the iron of Monarchism and fascism is mixed with the clay of democracy, socialism and communism. Daniel foresaw it all.
"And brake them to pieces"	This strikes the death blow to the evolutionists and the conversionists alike. The world is not to be converted by the preaching of the gospel. It is to be smashed to smithereens by the appearing of Christ as King.
"No place was found for them"	World Government is to be swept from the earth. Man's day and man's rule are to cease and God's day is to dawn. Man and man's government are incurably corrupt and must be swept away.
"The stone became a great mountain"	After world governments have been smitten and smashed, Christ will set up his millennial Kingdom of righteousness and peace.
"The stone filled the whole earth"	"Thy kingdom come" at last is answered. (1) Superhuman (cut out without hands) (2) Universal (filled the earth) (3) Perpetual (it shall stand for ever, v. 44)
"The Kingdom shall be divided" v. 41	We are now living in the era of the divided Roman empire. There is the iron rule or misrule of autocracy with the clay rule or misrule of democracy.
"The toes of the feet"	The tenfold division of the old Roman Empire was thus clearly foreseen by Daniel. The number TEN speaks of completeness, and hence a prophecy of complete division and

	disruption as well as a prophecy that in the end time ten kings shall rule the earth just prior to the apocalypse of Christ as King.
"They shall mingle themselves with the seed of men"	Here is a distinct prophecy of the breaking down of racial barriers. Kings were to mingle, mix with and marry peasants and races inter-mix, intermingle and inter-marry. This has been minutely fulfilled.
"But they shall not cleave one to another"	Unity impossible. A plain prophecy of the failure of League of Nations, World courts, World Monetary Conferences, World Disarmament Conferences, Peace Conferences and marriage of Royalty with commoners. All was foreseen clearly by Daniel. History is simply the fulfillment of prophecy. Prophecy sure sheds a lot of light on history.
"They shall not cleave"	Who or what can unite England and Ireland, France and Germany, Japan and Korea, Japan and China, Mohammedanism and Christians. The world empire of a united Babylon or Rome has passed and passed forever and neither the Napoleons nor the Kaisers of past, present or future can possibly unite them again. We challenge the world to either destroy the Jew, the Bible, or the Church, or bring about another world empire. The next world empire is to be the empire of Christ. Napoleon was doomed to failure by Daniel the prophet. Had the Kaiser of Germany understood Daniel he never would have attempted world dominion. The same applies to Mussolini, Hitler and Stalin, et al. We are now living in v. 43 of Dan. 2.

"In the days of these kings"	The ten kings as represented by the ten toes shall arise during the great tribulation.
"Shall the God of heaven set up a kingdom"	The next universal world empire shall be the empire of Christ which shall never be destroyed. "The dream is certain and the interpretation thereof sure" v. 45.

**THE IMAGE OF GOLD
THREE HOLY YOUNG MEN**

3

THE IMAGE OF GOLD

Nebuchadnezzar made an image of gold

World Wide Gentile Empires *began* with an image set up for the universal worship of man (Daniel 3). They will *end* with another image set up for the self same purpose (Rev. 13:14-15, etc.) A universal boycott together with a prominent mark and a death penalty for refusal to worship is the issue in each case. Beware of boycotts, dictators and marks (see "Riches From Revelation").

Nimrod was the first person to attempt to unify the religions of man by self deification. Nebuchadnezzar here attempts exactly the same thing and both were types of the coming "Beast" the last head of the Gentile world who will insist on being worshipped (Rev. 13:11-15; 19-20).

An image of gold

The Babylonian age was pre-eminently the golden age of human history. The king of Babylon made an image—a casting of gold of priceless value—an image that was probably intended by Satan to give the lie to Daniel's interpretation of deterioration, decay, devolution and ultimate destruction. It was an image bidding defiance to God and to his prophet.

The Plain of Dura

On the plains of Dura there stands today, a rectilinear mound, about twenty feet high, an exact square of about forty-six feet at the base, resembling the pedestal of a colossal statue. Everything leads to the belief that Nebuchadnezzar's golden image was set up in this place.

Nebuchadnezzar's proud and imperious personality has been stamped upon our imagination from childhood. The monuments bear abundant testimony to the same. "To astonish mankind, I reconstructed and renewed the wonder of Borsippa, the temple of the seven spheres of the world." The Arabs still use the ruins of Babylon as a large quarry, and carry off its bricks. Nine out of every ten of these bricks is stamped with the name of Nebuchadnezzar, a silent answer to the truth of his question "Is not this great Babylon which I have built?"

Whoso falleth not down

One of the characteristics of Gentile times is the deification of man. Satan attempted this in the garden of Eden, "Ye shall be as gods." Selah! Nimrod, inspired by Satan, attempted the same in the land of Shinar which resulted in the first Babylon.

Nebuchadnezzar endeavored to establish a religion of his own and a religion which was opposed to the God of heaven. He set up the image of a man. The image was sixty (6x10) cubits high and six cubits broad and six kinds of musical instruments called the crowd to worship. Thus the mysterious number 666 was stamped on the image of man set up by Nebuchadnezzar. This beginning of the "times of the Gentiles" also foreshadows its end as described in Rev. 13.

The civil power of the whole empire of Babylon tried to force this universal man-deifying religion upon the world just as in the latter days of the oncoming great tribulation, the devil, the Anti Christ and the false prophet, the triumvirate of hell, will force a false religion on the world. The Roman Cæsars each claimed Divine honors. The Emperor of Japan to this day claims divine honors and divine worship. Papal Rome has put a man up as vicegerent of the Lord, the Vicar of God, and foolish man stoops to kiss his toe. All about us we see the increasing deification of man and the humanizing of God. All this is to head up in a great apostasy and the revelation of the man of Sin, the coming Anti Christ, who will demand universal worship for himself (2 Thes. 2) (See "Riches from Revelation").

All the people fell down and worshipped

Gentile dominion and power is thus seen to be idolatrous, intolerant, self willed and blasphemous. It stands in direct opposition to God, repudiates the Sovereignty of the Almighty, is antagonistic to Christ and flings His followers into dens of lions or fiery furnaces. This Satan deluded world has always clubbed its Abels, mocked its Isaacs, imprisoned its Jeremiahs, beheaded its Johns and crucified its saviours.

A burning fiery furnace

Putting people to death in this way was not unusual in the East. For certain offences some were put upon a spit and roasted over a slow fire, and some were thrown into hot ovens. The three Hebrews were to be cast into a burning fiery furnace.

Have not regarded thee

To the three Hebrews, Nebuchadnezzar was not the last word. To them Nebuchadnezzar was neither divine nor supreme. They were neither afraid of Kings' faces nor fiery furnaces. May God raise up more young men like them. We need a few Shadrachs in our colleges today. God give us men.

His rage and fury

The greatness of the three Hebrew holy boys and the littleness of the Gentile unholy king is set forth in striking contrast in these two verses. The calmness of the godly young men presents a remarkable background for the rage and fury of the ruler. The three Holy Companions were the real rulers. They were the real kings.

Is it true?

Is it of purpose? Is it true, O Shadrach? The Hebrew youths refuse to acknowledge in any way any heathen religion. They determined to hold fast at any cost to the only true God and to the truth of God. They preferred death, disgrace and doom to apostasy or compromise.

Sackbut, psaltery, dulcimer

The sackbut was a triangular four stringed instrument, while the dulcimer was similar to the Scottish "Bagpipe." The dulcimer was probably a skin bag with two reed pipes while the psaltery was a stringed instrument.

Who is that God

The history of the Church has been written in the blood of its saints. There has always been warfare between the powers of darkness and light. The seed of the serpent and the seed of the woman have been in perpetual warfare ever since the fall of man. Among the noble army of martyrs, Abel leads the van and Cain appears as the first persecutor of God's saints. From that day to the present a sin loving world has labored to destroy the people of God.

Who is that God that shall deliver you

How blasphemous and God defying! Who is THAT GOD? asks the proud, pompous king. THAT God had recently honored him with a wonderful dream. THAT GOD had renewed the dream to Daniel. THAT GOD had graciously granted the interpretation. THAT GOD had made known the whole history of the world to him. WHO is THAT GOD? Oh, how wicked, wayward, and wilful is the heart of man!

THAT GOD had created him, protected him, provided for him, clothed him, fed him and honored him with rulership of the first world empire.

He little knew and little cared that his breath and being were in the hands of the one whom he is pleased to call THAT GOD.

Who shall deliver you out of my hands?

The ultimate trial of faith which sooner or later comes to all the saints is set forth in Daniel 1 and 3. From Abel, Isaac, Jacob, Moses, Daniel and the three Hebrews to John the Baptist, Paul, Luther, Wesley, Booth and Bresee to the present

THE IMAGE OF GOLD / 61

time, this Christ rejecting world has always persecuted its Pauls, despised its Daniels and slain its Saints.

We have no need to answer thee

To hesitate, argue, reason or parley with sin is fatal. Where the path of duty is plain, unhesitating decision and implicit obedience is the only safety. "We are not careful to answer thee." "We have no need to answer thee." The homage demanded of them was a POSITIVE homage, that demanded of Daniel was a NEGATIVE homage of abstaining from prayer. They would not yield to either!

We are not careful to answer thee

Principles were more to be regarded than policies. Their own personal safety was the least of their concern. They believed that "We ought to obey God" first, and then "honor the king." They practiced the principle later laid down in the New Testament that "We ought to obey God rather than men." Civil government is recognized in scripture as ordained of God for the civil welfare of men, and Christians are to be subject to the powers that be, whatever the form of government (Rom. 13:1-7). But when, as in Nebuchadnezzar's time, human law enters the realm of religion and commands disobedience to God's law, *duty to God comes first*. This lesson in civil government and religion, is important for our time, for, as Revelation 13 teaches, religious organizations in power are again seeking to use civil authority to coerce the conscience, in the effort to compel conformity to religious practices that are contrary to God's law.

We must say NO to kings and governments, parliaments and Senate's, when their will and commands are in conflict with the will and Word of God.

Our God is able

The two images of Daniel 2 and 3 represent man's rule and man's worship. The "image of Gold" was Nebuchadnezzar's "new thought" and "new theology." The king's unenlightened ingenuity set up a new object of worship. The loudly heralded musical attraction was all the more calculated to delude and fool the people, but God's holy people could not be so easily deceived. They preferred death to disobedience. They were fully persuaded as to God's power and presence and were possessed of implicit trust in his goodness and love.

But if not

Living or dying we are determined to be true to our God and His holy word.

Behold the courageous refusal of God's faithful three. Uttering no threatening words, guilty of no outrageous language and yet at the same time speaking no flatteries and making no soothing addresses, these holy youths calmly assured the king that they were by no means perplexed about the consequences. They needed no time even to pray about the matter. They were not even concerned about the event. One thing they had settled. They would on no account at any time worship any of his gods, compromise with conscience, or adore either the king or his image.

If not

This does not imply any inability on God's part. It is a question of His Will. If it is not the will of God to deliver us, we will not bow down. The three Hebrews preferred death to disobedience.

We will not

To Daniel and his holy Hebrew friends, truth had no latitude and loyalty to God no longitude.

Faithful to God and uncompromising with sin they are also a fit type of the Jewish remnant in the last days who will be faithful to God in the fiery furnace of the great tribulation. All these things are foreshadowings of events yet future (Rom. 15:4).

The flame slew those men

His pride wounded, his will crossed, and, his supposed supreme authority disregarded by three youths, Nebuchadnezzar resolved to take ample vengeance on them. The king's commandment was urgent. The furnace was made exceeding hot. The bodies of God's boys were fastened together. Strong soldiers flung them headlong into the flames. The fires which were intended for the children of God slew the soldiers.

Walking in the midst of the fire

Paul refused to walk out of prison (2 Cor. 12:8-9). Noah waited in the Ark till God ordered him to leave. Daniel was at home in the den of lions and these three Hebrews were in no hurry to get out of the fiery furnace. They were evidently enjoying the walk up and down in the midst of their fiery ordeal!

Four men loose

The fire simply burnt the cords with which they were bound and really set them at liberty. Our hearts may be enlarged by those very troubles with which enemies may desire to straiten, hamper and destroy us.

And they have no hurt

They made no complaint, felt no pain, experienced no uneasiness. The fire did not burn them, the flame did not scorch them, the smoke did not inconvenience them, and in them the scripture was literally fulfilled "When thou walkest through the fire thou shalt not be burned." "By faith . . . they quenched the violence of fire." The fourth in the midst suffered them not to be burned. Here is something undeniably supernatural. Jehovah had promised as though anticipating this very circumstance "When thou walkest through the fire thou shalt not be burned; neither shall the flame kindle upon thee." The loving Lord kept his promise to his trusting people. During the terrors of the great tribulation yet to come God's persecuted people will likewise be preserved. They were not saved FROM the fiery furnace, but they were saved IN it and preserved THROUGH it Selah!

The form of the fourth

Cast out by man they were thereby brought into a more beautiful fellowship with Christ. Paul, Silas, Bunyan, and a multitude of others have been cast out into the arms of a waiting Christ.

The fourth . . . the Son of God

Christ came down to deliver Daniel from the lions' den and the three Hebrews from the fiery furnace.

HE CAME DOWN and linked arms with Adam and Eve in the Garden of Eden.

HE CAME DOWN and walked with Enoch.

HE CAME DOWN and talked with Noah.

HE CAME DOWN and feasted with Abraham.

HE CAME DOWN and wrestled with Jacob.

HE CAME DOWN and manifested himself to Moses.

HE CAME DOWN and filled the tabernacle in the wilderness and the temple.

HE CAME DOWN and REVEALED the will of God to Gideon and Manoah.

HE CAME DOWN and GUIDED Israel through the wilderness.

HE CAME DOWN and DEFENDED Israel as Captain of the Lord's hosts.

HE CAME DOWN and DELIVERED Daniel from the den of the lions and the three Hebrews from the fiery furnace and finally HE CAME DOWN and was born in a stable and cradled in a manger—God manifested in the flesh. Oh the condescension of Christ. Oh the goodness, greatness and grace of God.

The same Christ who appeared to Adam in Eden, who walked with Enoch and talked with Noah, who wrestled with

Jacob and feasted with Abraham, who appeared to Moses in the burning bush and to Joshua on the walls of Jericho, again stepped from the heavenly portals and entered the fiery furnace to succor and support his faithful followers. The form of the fourth is always in the midst of His holy people.

And have changed the king's word

Kings and presidents, together with their decrees, are all in the hands of the Jehovah of the Old Testament. The Pharaohs and Nebuchadnezzars of the past and present may determine the destruction of God's people but blessed be the God of Israel, Daniel and Shadrach! He is able to change the damnable decrees of mad monarchs and take care of His own.

And yielded their bodies

One reason why God protected and preserved them was because they were wholly and absolutely His own. They had yielded themselves to God (Rom. 12:1-2). Their consecration was complete and they were therefore immortal until their work was done.

Shall be cut in pieces

Nebuchadnezzar was convinced but not converted and transformed. God did not inspire Nebuchadnezzar to use these words, but having uttered them the Holy Spirit inspired Daniel to record them. The saying of wicked demons or bad men were not inspired by God although God was pleased to inspire the writers to record same. The sayings of Satan, as in Gen. 3:1 were not inspired by God, but God inspired Moses to write them and hence they are part of the inspired scriptures. Nebuchadnezzar was still the same old cruel despot ready to cut in pieces his own people! What madness.

Then the king promoted Shadrach

The secret of success is obedience to God and His word. Uncompromising devotion to God and unbending conformity to His word are at once the way to both peace and prosperity.

Their faithfulness to God and His word was richly rewarded. They were each given a larger sphere and a new opportunity for bigger service to king and country. They had passed from death (the furnace) unto life (Christ) and as a consequence they were privileged to bear a greater witness. The king promoted them.

> "Standing by a purpose true,
>   Heeding God's command,
> Honor them, the faithful few!
>   All hail to Daniel's Band!

Dare to be a Daniel! dare to stand alone!
Dare to have a purpose firm! dare to make it known!

> Many mighty men are lost,
>   Daring not to stand,
> Who for God has been a host,
>   By joining Daniel's Band.
>
> Many giants, great and tall,
>   Stalking through the land,
> Headlong to the earth would fall,
>   If met by Daniel's Band!
>
> Hold the Gospel banner high!
>   On to victory grand!
> Satan and his host defy,
>   And shout for Daniel's Band!"

THE CONVERSION
OF A KING

4

CONVERSION OF A KING

**The Dream of Nebuchadnezzar
The tree in the midst of the earth
The Key**

"It is thou, O king" 4:22.

The Vision
4:10-17

"Behold a tree"
"In the midst of the earth"

"The height thereof was great"

"The tree grew and was strong"

"The sight thereof to the end of all the earth"
"The leaves thereof were fair"

"The fruit thereof much"

"In it was meat for all"

"The beasts of the field had shadow under it"
"All flesh was fed on it"
"Behold a watcher"
"An holy one"

"Hew down the tree"
"Cut off his branches"
"Shake off his leaves"
"Scatter his fruit"
"Let the beasts get away and the fowls"
"Nevertheless leave the stump"

The Interpretation
4:18-37

Nebuchadnezzar
World empire of Babylon under Nebuchadnezzar
The greatness, grandeur and glory of Nebuchadnezzar and his empire
"It is thou, O King, that art grown and become strong"
The universal world empire of Babylon
Handsome men and beautiful women
The children of Nebuchadnezzar. Princes and Princesses
Self contained and independent. Like the U.S.A. rather than like England which is dependent upon others for national sustenance.
Man and beast protected and preserved.
World wide trade and commerce
A holy unfallen angel
Another holy unfallen spirit intelligence of a different order and office
The ruin of Nebuchadnezzar
Dominions and dependencies
Loss of his subjects
His children
Protection gone

Neither Nebuchadnezzar nor his kingdom were to be utterly ruined or completely destroyed

"Even with a band of iron and brass"	The kingdom was to be left and preserved unto him after judgment had done its work.
"Let it be wet with the dew of heaven"	Nebuchadnezzar to be homeless and shelterless
"Let his portion be with the beasts"	Reason was to take wings, fly away and leave him as an irrational, senseless, irresponsible beast.
"Lt a beast's heart be given unto him"	Nebuchadnezzar was to become bestial, without a conscience and without reason. Caring only for self, gratifying the senses and spending his existence regardless of God or the future, all of which is characteristic of a beast
"Let seven times pass over him"	For seven years he was to imagine himself a beast of the field and eat grass like an ox
"His hairs were grown like eagles' feathers and his nails like birds' claws"	It is a fearful thing to fall into the hands of the living God. Those who walk in pride God is able to abase.

No secret troubleth thee (4:9)

How blessed! Mysteries on every hand but not to *trouble* the humble, holy, children of God. We know that all things work together for good and hence the providences of God do not *trouble* us. We know that God is too wise to err and too good to be unkind and hence trials and tests, suffering and sorrow, bereavement and loss do not *trouble* us. We do not ask God, why? for no secret *troubleth* the saints. Let not your heart be *troubled*. God's children may discover from direct sources every secret which is right, proper and beneficial for them to have and know.

This matter is by the decree of the watchers

The watchers are heavenly, angelic messengers watching over the affairs of men. Important decisions affecting the welfare of men are here stated to be in the hands of these superintending unfallen spirit princes. All angels are ministering spirits. These watchers however, make decrees and execute them. The flourishing tree, setting forth the power, fame, wealth and prosperity of Nebuchadnezzar was to be cut down and the cutting down was the direct decision and decree of the angelic watchers.

The decree of the watchers

These holy, heavenly beings are ever on the watch to execute the will and word of God. In the great and good government of God there are not only millions of unfallen ministering spirits, but there are special angels who render special service for God and humanity. Michael, the archangel, has special jurisdiction over the Jews while Gabriel seems supremely concerned for the Gentiles. There are also Cherubim and Seraphim, Morning Stars, Sons of the Morning, Sons of God and also an innumerable host of angels. Then there is another special order of spirit intelligences called WATCHERS. These WATCHERS under God have power to issue decrees and order the execution of the same. "FULL of eyes within and without they rest not day nor night." They are special WATCHERS over the affairs of men and are set to take care of the interests of God's government on earth. They watched the doings of Nebuchadnezzar and when his pride and insolence reached a certain limit they demanded judgment upon him. They had WATCHED over Abraham for good and over Sodom for evil and when Sodom's cup was full judgment fell. They had WATCHED over Lot for good and even pulled him out of the doomed city. They WATCHED over Nebuchadnezzar for good but when his sin reached its limit they determined a decree and demanded his doom.

The veil which hides the unseen world from our sight is again lifted for a moment as it is often lifted both in Daniel and Revelation. The WATCHERS refer to a heavenly court of angels interested only in the performance of the plans of God. The Judicial Court of Watchers or Holy Ones are a part of the great and glorious Divine organization and kingdom. The Judgment which came upon the king was according to the sentence of the heavenly seers and the word of the holy watchers. The study of Angelology is an important study and no student of the scriptures can afford to remain in ignorance concerning the constant activity of angels.

The WATCHERS demand the punishment of Nebuchadnezzar. They plead against him for his pride and impenitence. They decree his humiliation and judgment and Jehovah God agrees and consents to the justice and righteousness of their demands and Nebuchadnezzar's doom is sealed. The decree of the watchers, the word of the holy ones, becomes the decree of the most High and Nebuchadnezzar was doomed. How dreadful to have holy angels plead against us because of our pride and wicked ways.

The basest—of men

God orders the events and disposes the destinies of men. He brings low and lifts up. He raises the beggar from the dung hill to set him among princes (1 Sam. 2:8-9). He exalts the lowly and abases the proud and ruleth in the kingdom of men and giveth it to whomsoever he will and setteth up over it the basest of men.

It is thou

"Thou art the man." The prophet speaks plainly and pointedly. There was no circumlocution. There was no trimming the edges or rounding the corners. There was no flattery. "It is thou O King." While we may not rant, rage, or fume against sinners under a pretext of being hot or zealous we must not on the other hand use flattering words and compromise with sin under the pretext of winning sinners to the church, or keeping the young people. We must not play politics, but we may use tact and moderation.

Break off thy sins

Repent. Repent ye. Throughout the pages of scripture there is a steady constant insistence on repentance. The Bible is indeed a handbook on repentance. Repentance is commanded, urged, enforced and illustrated. Over 60 times the

New Testament alone enforces the necessity of repentance. The great doctrine of Repentance occupies a pre-eminent place in the teaching of Christ and His inspired Apostles. The first recorded utterance of the fore-runner of Christ was REPENT (Matt. 3:2). The first recorded word in the ministry of the Master Himself was REPENT (Matt. 4:17). When Peter was asked by the convicted crowd after the Day of Pentecost "What shall we do?" Peter's first word was REPENT (Acts 2:37-39). There is no such thing as experiential Salvation or Sanctification apart from repentance. There is no such thing as vital communion or fellowship with God without repentance. The business of the God called and God ordained preacher is not to preach smooth things but saving things. It is not that which we WANT to hear, but that which we OUGHT to hear. We must not tone down the truth just to get people to join church. The standard of truth must not be lowered simply to obtain a few extra silver dollars or dimes. God Almighty has given us His last Word. The last WORD is Christ and Christ's first word is REPENT. "At sundry times and in divers manners God spake in times past," but now God speaks to us through His son and the word of THE SON OF GOD is REPENT. The soul of man is in anarchy, the will of man is in rebellion and in fact the whole man by nature is against God, Christ and Holiness and hence the necessity of repentance. "Break off thy sins."

The first word of God to sinful man then is REPENT. Some of us are getting sick and tired of hearing the parrot cry of "Only believe, . . . Only believe." Devils believe and then tremble, but they remain devils. Demons know that Christ is the Son of God, but they remain demons. Men are not in any condition of heart to believe until after conviction and repentance. Both conviction and repentance must precede the step of faith which saves the soul. "Break off thy sins" is the burden of both Testaments. If preaching that men should "repent" is too sensational, startling or vulgar then it is God's vulgarity. John Baptist was pushed into prison because he preached repentance, but no sooner was the voice of John stilled than the voice of Jesus was heard continuing the message exactly where John stopped and that message was REPENT. If repentance is shallow the Christian life will be shallow. Sin, the world and the devil must be forsaken or Christ cannot be received. "Break off thy sins."

Repentance is more than conviction. Conviction is being awakened while repentance is getting up and getting out. Repentance is more than SORROW. Weeping at funerals and sentimental plays and sissy songs is not repentance. Singing on Sunday either in church or home will not save the sinful soul of man. The outstanding illustration of true repentance is to be found in the sublime story of the prodigal son. He left the whole sickening, hoggish business of sin and never stopped until he was in the father's arms and father's home. That is repentance.

A lengthening of thy tranquillity

In loving loyalty to God and to the King, Daniel beseeches Nebuchadnezzar to repent and break off his sins by righteousness that perchance in the good providence of God the stroke of divine wrath about to fall might be withheld.

At the end of twelve months

These twelve months were months of grace in which Nebuchadnezzar was given opportunity to break off his sins. All things, however, continued as before and God's warnings together with the earnest exhortation of God's Prophet were neglected and forgotten. Nebuchadnezzar glorified his own great Babylon and while the words were in his mouth a voice from heaven declared his doom. Pride goeth before a fall. Nebuchadnezzar's lust for pomp and power ended in lunacy.

Twelve months

Twelve months' grace was given. He was to be left without excuse. The lengthening of his tranquillity and the continuation of his present prosperity depended on his penitence.

120 years of respite was granted to the antediluvians without avail and now twelve months are granted to Nebuchadnezzar also without avail. The goodness of God failed to lead them to repentance. The grace of God was given in vain to the Sons of Cain (Gen. 6:3) to Ahab (1 Kings 21:27) and to Nebuchadnezzar (Dan. 4:20).

Is not this great Babylon which I

The king's soul was filled with pride and self-idolatry. Instead of being penitent and humble he is high minded and haughty. While the arrogant words were on his lips the terrible voice of doom fell upon his rebellious ear and stubborn heart. The king's success in making Babylon the wonder of the world was employed to feed the fires of his imperial vanity. He forgot he was made of dust and therefore mortal. He also forgot that he was accountable to a higher power. While the boastful and blasphemous words were on his lips the sword of justice and judgment fell. Bereft of reason and utterly neglected and despised, for seven long years he lived as a beast of the field. Driven from men he ate grass as an ox till his hairs were grown like eagles' feathers and his nails like birds' claws.

I . . . my . . . my

The five times repeated "I" of Lucifer introduced sin in the universe of God. The four times repeated "I" of Pharaoh placed him in direct antagonism to God and Israel and the impious opposition of Nebuchadnezzar with his egotistical "I" and "My" brought swift retribution upon him as it did upon Pharaoh and Lucifer before him.

His nails like . . . claws

Punished with madness and fancying himself a beast, Nebuchadnezzar, the great king of Babylon walked out of the Palace on all fours and for seven years was a fit subject for an asylum for the insane. It does not pay to go against God.

Nebuchadnezzar by no means has been the only person to

become insane because of refusal to break with sin. If the truthful biography of insane people could be written what a volume it would be.

Lifted up mine eyes to heaven

The voice had issued from heaven (v. 31) and his reason left him. His mental derangement had annihilated seven years of his life so that when reason returned he remembered only the event that immediately preceded his insanity and hence he lifted up his eyes toward heaven. Having robbed God of His honor and having in turn been robbed of his reason, now that he has been healed, he looks up, praises and honors God whose great goodness had restored his reason. The restored king is so thankful to God that he heaps words upon words in praise of God whose providence had both punished and purified him (4:34-37).

Mine understanding returned unto me

Nebuchadnezzar awakened to find himself living the life of a beast. His friends might have cut his hair and clipped his nails, but without understanding he would have remained in the field. Outward reformation, water baptism, confirmation and church membership are not enough. The prodigal must first come to himself or else remain a prodigal.

What doest thou?

The awakened, healed and restored king here rises into a true apprehension of the God of the Bible (1) Most High (2) Ever living (3) Sovereign Ruler (4) Omnipotent (5) Righteous "None can ... say ... what doest thou?" for all his ways are right.

Those who walk in pride He is able to abase

After his return to reason and to rule, Nebuchadnezzar becomes a preacher. He declares a truth well worth remembering today. Back, as from the dead, he warns all future generations against pride. Back as from the grave he preaches the virtues and blessings of humility for "Those who walk in pride God is able to abase."

**DRINKING AND DANCING
ON THE VERGE OF DOOM**

5

DRINKING AND DANCING

Belshazzar the king

The search for buried records in the ruins of old Babylonia has brought to light a cylinder tablet with a brief record of the taking of Babylon by the forces of the Medes and Persians, in the year 538 B.C. This record shows that "in the month Tammuz" (June) the troops of Cyrus defeated King Nabonidus in the open country, and then entered Babylon "without battle." (The ancient Greek historians say that Cyrus drained off the river Euphrates which ran through the city so that his troops were able to enter beneath the walls, along the bed of the river). Evidently the inner citadel, which was a walled, fort-like enclosure with great temples and palaces, held out, under the king's son Belshazzar. For several months this inner citadel resisted; and then, the broken tablet tells us, "in the night of the 11th day of Marchisvan" (October) the general in command made attack "Against . . . " (the writing being here defaced) evidently the citadel. In this attack, "he slew the king's son." Thus the broken tablet tells in a fragmentary way of that last night of Belshazzar's feast, so long told in its fulness by the inspired pen of the prophet. Because ancient history had never mentioned Belshazzar, critics had claimed that the record in Daniel was not true. But the ancient tablets dug up from the sands have silenced this criticism.

The three tablets of Belshazzar which the spade of the Archeologists have brought to light have fully established the identity of Belshazzar the king, routed the higher critics, and incidentally vindicated the veracity of the prophet Daniel.

The golden and silver vessels

According to Chapter one these vessels were carried by Nebuchadnezzar into the temple of his god, Bel. In his drunken frolic and frenzy Belshazzar commanded them to be brought and filled with liquor, thus adding insult to injury. This profanation of sacred things was the filling up of the king's cup of wickedness and brought swift judgment from God.

They drank wine and praised the gods

Drunkenness and idolatry go hand in hand. There are more gods in Japan than there are Japanese to worship them. There are at least 300 million gods in India. Man is a worshipper. Man is religious and must worship God or gods.

Upon the plaster of the wall of the king's palace:

The victories, exploits and glories of kings and empires were written upon the walls of the king's palace in order to remind all who entered of the regal splendour.

The hand that wrote

The same divine hand which had previously written the two tablets of the law for God's people, the same divine hand which later wrote on the ground in defense of a poor fallen, but penitent woman, now writes the death knell of Belshazzar and proclaims his doom. Without previous warning, without being accompanied by terrifying thunder and lightning, the judgment of God fell and Belshazzar was slain. The profanation of sacred things brings down the swift displeasure of Jehovah. Sometimes God's judgments may be slow, but sometimes they may be surprisingly swift and sudden.

The joints of his loins were loosed

Four things are here declared about the profane king. (1) His countenance was changed (2) His thoughts troubled him (3) The joints of his loins were loosed (4) His knees smote one against another. Despair swept over the drunken despot. Death, doom and damnation were just around the corner. In one brief hour the boastful, profane king becomes a shivering, shaking, helpless and hopeless mortal. He came up against the bosses of Jehovah's buckler and was broken.

The king cried aloud

If Belshazzar had never been in earnest before he was surely in earnest now. If he had never been in haste before he was certainly in haste now. If he had never been afraid before he was unmistakably afraid now. "The king cried aloud." Unknown to him, he was within three feet from death and within twenty-four hours from the grave and hell. The measure of his days was finished, his cup of iniquity was full and his doom was fixed.

Clothed with scarlet

Gold chains and scarlet robes were only bestowed on the most meritorious persons. The vain heart of man delights in the wearing of such fantastic things. What a sight it must be to angels and devils to see human beings strutting around with lodge relics, royal robes, mayoralty chains, gold and glass necklaces and the whole catalogue of fiddle-de-dees and fol-de-rols. I wonder what Belshazzar thinks of scarlet robes and gold chains now? I wonder what Nebuchadnezzar thinks of his once glorious Babylon now? I wonder what Nimrod thinks of his tower building project now? May the good Lord help us to see the childishness and vanity of chains of gold and clothes of scarlet and everything else that ministers to human pride and haughtiness.

The queen . . . said O King

During the regime and reign of Belshazzar Daniel had evidently been forgotten. He was probably set aside by the pleasure-loving, lustful lords and ladies. He was now of little or no use to them and was certainly not employed in any high office or department of state. The queen, however, remembered his past service to his king and country and in an hour of tremendous need the queen entered the banqueting hall and addressed the king reminding him that there was a man in his kingdom through whom there may be given wisdom, light and understanding. At the right time God had the right man ready.

Dissolving of doubts

The word translated doubts may also be translated KNOTS. Daniel was an unraveler of knots. The world is in desperate need of men who are dissolvers of doubts. World problems are puzzling and baffling the brains of the greatest statesmen on earth. Oh for heaven-born, heaven-sent Daniels, both in churches, and nations.

The third ruler in the kingdom

In 1854 Sir Henry Rawlinson translated a number of tablets which were brought to light by the spade of the archeologist. These tablets contain the name of Belshazzar, establish the existence of the king of Babylon and of course incidentally settle the question of the dependability of the Book of Daniel. From the expression "The third ruler of the kingdom" it is more than likely that Belshazzar shared the government with some other monarch in much the same way as Darius and Cyrus later jointly ruled over the affairs of Babylon. Belshazzar evidently thought of himself as the second ruler and therefore promised Daniel the third place in the kingdom. Belshazzar was evidently a joint ruler with his more illustrious father. Had he been the only monarch Daniel would have been second instead of third.

Let thy gifts be to thyself

The now highly commercialized custom of giving and receiving has become a great evil. Christmas giving and receiving as now practiced by Christians has robbed many a heathen soul of his only chance of peace here and salvation hereafter. Daniel was unconcerned about gifts for himself. He was careless about earthly rewards. He knew that gifts blinded the receiver and he refused to be blinded.

Nebuchadnezzar thy father . . . thou his son

Critics both past and present have attempted to discredit Daniel because he calls Belshazzar the son of Nebuchadnezzar.

When it is remembered however, that in the Semitic language as also in some Oriental languages there is no name for grandson and grandfather the boomerang returns to the critic's cranium. Mephibosheth is called the son of Saul in the same way that Belshazzar is called the son of Nebuchadnezzar. It may either mean son or grandson. The neighbours of Naomi as recorded in the book of Ruth (4:17) said 'There is a SON born to Naomi." The word means either a son or grandson. The son was born to Ruth and hence was the grandson of Naomi. All missionaries in the Orient are familiar with these Oriental expressions. No one misunderstands them except the critics. In fact, "Son" in the Oriental lands may be either SON or GRANDSON or GREAT-GRANDSON. Mephibosheth is called the son of Saul whereas he was really the son of Jonathan and the grandson of Saul. Obed is called the son of Naomi whereas in reality he was the son of Ruth and hence the grandson of Naomi. The twelve tribes beginning with Reuben and ending with Benjamin are all said to be sons of Abraham whereas they were sons of Jacob and great-grandsons of Abraham. Even in the New Testament Lazarus is called the son of Abraham. "Son" therefore may be son, grandson, descendant or offspring. It is still common in the East to call any ancestor "Father" and any descendant "Son." To this day Christians, Jews and Mohammedams claim Abraham as their father. We are all SONS of Adam and may become sons of Abraham and SONS of God by the new birth and then we may follow the steps of that faith of our father Abraham. Blind unbelief is sure to err.

Thou . . . hast not humbled thine heart

The judgments of God are intended to humble the hearts of men. Judgment is God's strange work. All God's dealings with man are intended to lead him to repentance and redemption. God's wrath upon Nebuchadnezzar was intended for his own good and should have been a warning to Belshazzar.

Though thou knewest all this

Sins against knowledge, experience, and example are the worst of sins and have the highest aggravation and culpability. Nebuchadnezzar was dreadfully punished for his pride and Belshazzar knew all this. Example and warning alike failed to impress the impious Belshazzar and hence his sin was great and his judgment speedy. If we sin wilfully after receiving knowledge of the truth there remaineth no more sacrifice for sin.

> There is a line by us unseen
> That crosses every path
> The hidden boundary between
> God's mercy and his wrath.

Belshazzar sinned against light, hardened his heart, and stiffened his neck and was cut off without remedy. He knew about the pride of his predecessor, he knew how God had humiliated him and degraded him by depriving him of human reason and conscience, he knew that God had restored the mad monarch and had given back to him his dominion, power and glory, he knew of the edict of praise issued by the humbled Nebuchadnezzar, he knew all this and hence sinned against light and knowledge. He loved darkness rather than light and died in his sin. He loved sin rather than holiness and died without hope. Weighed and wanting he went to his own place.

God . . . hast thou not glorified

Man was created to glorify God and enjoy Him forever. Belshazzar refused to humble his heart before God, sought only his own pleasure and glory and accordingly perished. The hidden purposes of God were again revealed to God's holy prophet and through the prophet made known to the king. Without a word of warning, entreaty or exhortation Daniel pronounced the doom of the drunken monarch. Instead of proclaiming "a day of national humiliation, fasting and prayer" and devoutly recognizing the "supreme authority and just government of Almighty God," Belshazzar made a great feast and drank wine before the thousands, and forgetful of God and His glory that night he was slain.

Feasting and falling very often go hand in hand. Daniel's fasting, self-denial and abstinence even in things lawful and legitimate in themselves contributed much toward his staunch, good and great character while Belshazzar's feasts and frolics accomplished his fall and ruin. The third step in the downfall of Samson was the making of a feast at which he invited thirty godless young men. We need to beware of our dinner parties, social feastings and fun making masqueradings. The devil is not dead and seven spirits more satanic than the one cast out in sanctification are awaiting an opportunity to enter and possess the saints of God. We must fast, watch and pray or Satan will deceive us and bring about our fall and ruin.

And God hast thou not glorified

Man was created for the glory of God and his own eternal good and happiness. Belshazzar lifted up himself against the Lord of heaven, lived for selfish pleasure and in defiance of God. Without any exhortation to repentance or amendment of life Daniel pronounced his doom. In the channel of the river Cyrus marched his host into the city and that night Belshazzar was slain.

Mene, mene, tekel, upharsin

Mene means numbered and finished. Tekel means weighed and wanting. Upharsin means to divide or is now dividing and separating (present). Peres means divided and separated (past). Between the writing and the interpretation the words were fulfilled. Between the prophecy and the explanation the divine judgment fell and the prophecy fulfilled. The change of words from *Upharsin,* which means *dividing* and *Peres,* which means *divided,* the work was done. The Medes and Persians were at the gates and the weighed and wanting, wilful and wicked Belshazzar lost his kingdom, lost his life, lost his soul and his all. Sin ends in doom, death and hell.

Thou art weighed . . . and . . . wanting

A man once made a beautiful goblet. A serpent with gleaming eyes and open mouth was coiled up at the bottom. The death dealing fang was ready to sting the drinker who might empty the cup. Such is sin and its pleasures. Inflamed with wine, Belshazzar defied God, defiled God's holy things, lifted himself up against Jehovah and perished in his uncleanness. In the midst of a drunken carousal, the mysterious handwriting was seen upon the wall 'Mene, Mene, Tekel, Upharsin." Yes! God weighs kingdoms and kings. By His own will He sets up or flings down. God help us to submit to Him before it is too late.

Weighed . . . and . . . wanting

Daniel exhibited none of the sympathy for Belshazzar which he had previously shown for Nebuchadnezzar. The wilfulness, wickedness and recklessness of Belshazzar is revealed by him (1) Drinking to excess before his own subjects. (2) Profaning the sacred vessels of Jehovah. (3) Drinking before his wives and concubines who were usually not present at feasts in the East where females were kept in strict seclusion. As the reckless revelry advanced, the women were evidently introduced, and, unlike Vashti, they were willing to show themselves. (4) Persisting in their profanity they praised the gods of silver and gold and in the same hour God's displeasure was declared.

That night was Belshazzar slain

It is at once interesting and instructive to notice certain prophecies relating to the oppressors of God's people and the defiers of God's will.

(1) Egypt—The ancient world power of Egypt has been degraded and is now "the basest of kingdoms." Under British protection it is however being saved from utter extinction.

(2) Tyre:—The Liverpool, Southampton and New York of the ancient world. Tyre, whose sailors ventured into unknown seas carrying their commerce—where is she now? Where is Egypt? Where is Tyre?

(3) Babylon:—Behind the magnificent and wonderful walls and gorgeous gates of Babylon the profligate king laughed at the approach of Cyrus. The Divine fiat however, had gone forth, the soldiers of Cyrus entered the Palace and that night Belshazzar was slain. Where is Egypt? Tyre? Babylon? Sodom? Nineveh? They defied God and were debased and destroyed.

In that night

There was a last night in the history of Belshazzar. There is a last night to everything and everyone on earth. A last feast, a last fight, a last dance, a last movie, a last cigar, a last drink, a last cigarette, a last oath, a last supper, a last night. Your last night is at hand. Your last night is much nearer than you expect or think. Tonight may be your last night. It may also be a night without a morning as in the case of Belshazzar. The Belshazzars of today may make their great feasts, drink their expensive wines, profane holy things and mock holy men, but there is a last night for them all.

DANIEL IN THE LION'S DEN

6

DANIEL IN THE LION'S DEN

The presidents and princes against Daniel

These rivals of Machiavellian principles and practices determined to displace Daniel. The devil has always been against God's Daniels and has always sought their defeat and destruction. Only three things saved the day for Daniel, (1) His past life of peace and purity, (2) His present unswerving loyalty to God, (3) He believed in his God. (Verses 4, 16, 20, 23).

The deliverance of Daniel was a distinct foreshadowing of the coming deliverance of the faithful remnant in the last days of the Anti-Christ.

Daniel was first

Daniel was placed at the helm of the ship of state. Chancellor of the Exchequer and Prime Minister he was indeed first. Daniel honored God and God exalted Daniel.

We shall not find any occasion against this Daniel

The enemies of Daniel thus witnessed to the unsullied purity of his life. Daniel's character was invulnerable and his conduct unimpeachable. Even in the minute details of his arduous, busy, state life, he was faultless. His daily life, which always provides the severest test of character was exemplary, sweet, clean and pure.

There were probably other Daniels, but the integrity of THIS DANIEL was undoubted. Daniel's piety, holiness and integrity were his strong points. Never was a loftier tribute paid to mortal man than the enemies of Daniel paid to him that day. What a tremendous tribute to the trustworthiness of this public servant! The religion of Daniel operated with such power as to exclude everything in his conduct which might furnish a handle with which he might be accused and justly hurt.

All the presidents
What a lie! Daniel himself was the chief president, and he was not consulted!

Save of thee O king
This decree, which stated that "whosoever shall make a petition of any God or man for thirty days save of thee O King" was a means of flattering the king, but the real sinister object was the destruction of Daniel.

His window being open
He did not open his windows and hence there was no presumption. He did not close his windows and hence there was no cowardice. Cornelius was a man that prayed in his own house (Acts 10:30) and Daniel went into his house, kneeled and prayed three times a day. Watch and pray.

He kneeled
This is the most proper gesture in prayer. It is most expressive of humility, reverence and submission to God and His will. Kneeling is a begging posture and we must all come to God as beggars. He kneeled.

The king . . . was sore displeased
Daniel's preferment created jealousy. A cunning plan was devised and the king was deceived into signing the decree. Daniel's enemies were satisfied that his doom was sealed. When Darius discovered exactly what had been done he was sorely displeased with himself and set his heart on Daniel to deliver him, but all in vain. The law was passed and irrevocable. Darius labored all day to deliver Daniel, but the law stood squarely against him. Darius could find no way to deliver. What a contrast with the God of the Bible. God's holy law condemns man and condemns him justly, but God so loved the world that he found a way to save. Bless His name! God found a way to deliver!

The decree of Darius was a faint foreshadowing of another decree of a greater than Darius who in the end time will forbid any to worship anyone but himself.

The law of the Medes

The plotters got their law on the statute books, and then argued that because it was law, it must be enforced, right or wrong. That was the argument of those who crucified Jesus. "We have a law" said the plotters, "and by our law He ought to die" (John 19:7). Religious persecution has usually wrought its iniquities in the name of law.

Daniel refused to fuss, fight, fume or become furious. He calmly and quietly trusted in His God and made up his mind to obey God and an enlightened conscience. His own safety was his least concern. Selah!

The king sealed it with his own signet

This was done to tie the hands of the king so it might not be in his power to change the purpose concerning Daniel.

And with the signet of his lords

Neither the king nor parliament could help themselves once it was sealed. The decree was sealed not only with the signet of the sovereign ruler, but with the signet of his satraps so that it might not be in the power of either to save Daniel. The deliverance of Daniel must therefore be the sole work of Daniel's God.

Is thy God whom thou servest continually

Whom thou servest continually. Continually. Most of us serve God by spasms—but WHOM THOU SERVEST CONTINUALLY . . . In times of affliction and adversity as well as in plenty and prosperity. In times of persecution as well as times of peace. In times of sickness and helplessness as well as in times of health. In times of pain and poverty as well as in times of peace and plenty. "Whom thou servest continually."

My God hath shut the lions' mouths

These sublime stories reveal the channels through which God flashed his light and truth upon kings and peoples. Through Daniel and those who were associated with him kings and kingdoms saw the wisdom, power and presence of God. *Separated from* all the things in the midst of which they lived which were contrary to the will of God, *inspired* by living in fellowship with God and thus coming to understand the mind of God, *enabled* by divine power to proclaim the truth without fear or favour, these Holy Youths were instruments through whom God was able to make kings and courts feel the spell of his sovereign power. The distracted king asked Daniel if his God was able to deliver him and Daniel quickly replied "My God is not only able *but* He has done it." To Daniel, God was a personal, friendly, powerful, and present God.

Before thee have I done no wrong

The disobedience of Daniel was not because of any contempt for the king, but because of his regard to the King of Kings. To disobey kings, presidents and governors may sometimes become the duty of Christians for the Christian's first duty is to *Obey God* and *then* honor the king (Acts 24:16).

Because he believed in his God

Here is given the key to Daniel's deliverance from the den of lions. *Not* because he was a special favorite of Deity. *Not* because he was one of God's pets. *Not* because of any election, foreordination or predestination, but because he *believed*, because he *believed* in HIS GOD.

Enoch was translated because he believed in his God (Heb. 11:5). Abel offered a more excellent sacrifice than Cain because he believed in His God (Heb. 11:4). Noah built an ark to the saving of himself and his house because he believed in his God (Heb. 11:7). Abraham went out, not knowing whither he went because he believed in his God (Heb. 11:8). Joseph gave commandment concerning his bones because he believed in his God (Heb. 11:22). Moses *refused* to be called the son of Pharaoh's daughter, *choosing* rather to suffer affliction with the people of God, because he believed in his God, and Daniel ... stopped the mouths of lions because he believed in his God. (Heb. 11:32-33).

Cast them into the den of lions

It does not pay to fight against God or seek the hurt of God's people. Daniel's accusers were cast into the den of lions and destroyed. Destruction is awaiting all who falsely accuse the people of God.

The lions brake all their bones

Here is another example of democratic savagery and cruelty. The Medes and Persians were undoubtedly more socialistic and democratic than the Babylonians, but they were as savage, fierce and cruel as the most ultramonarchists and plutocrats. Whether Monarchies or Democracies, republicans or socialists, they are all the same at heart. Intrigue, jealousy, murder, envy, hatred of God and holiness, oppression and cruelty are characteristic of Gentile rule. Christ is earth's rightful king and theocracy the only beneficent government.

Brake all their bones in pieces

Daniel was unharmed, but before his accusers touched the floor of the den the hungry lions pounced upon them and smashed their bones in pieces. Here is a plain proof if such is needed that their not devouring Daniel was not through fulness or want of appetite which the higher critics would undoubtedly have affirmed but for this record.

The triumph of the wicked is short. They digged a pit for Daniel and they themselves were flung into it and destroyed. They erected a gallows upon which they perished. This is the inevitable end of all enemies of God and his saints. It does not pay to seek the hurt of God's people.

So this Daniel prospered

There may have been other Daniels who did less praying and praising, and who in turn escaped the persistent persecutions of their enemies, but *this* Daniel prayed, *this* Daniel praised, *this* Daniel persistently served God. *This* Daniel was *persecuted, this* Daniel was *protected, preserved, preferred* and *prospered.*

(1) He prayed. "He kneeled and prayed three times a day." (2) He praised, "and gave thanks." (3) He was persistent "whom thou servest continually." (4) He was persecuted. "That Daniel." (5) He was protected "Shut the lions mouths." (6) He was preferred "This Daniel was preferred." (7) He prospered "So this Daniel prospered." Cp "THAT Daniel" of 6:13 with "THIS Daniel" of 6:28.

Cyrus the Persian

With the rise of Cyrus there came into power the second of the *five* prophesied world empires. Cyrus was prophetically named more than a hundred years before he was born (Isa. 44:28, 45:1-4).

The five prophesied world empires (1) Babylon (2) Medes and Persians (3) Greece (4) Rome (5) Christ's Millennial kingdom.

THE FOUR GREAT BEASTS

7

THE FOUR GREAT BEASTS

In the first year of Belshazzar

The remaining portion of this most marvelous book consists of Daniel's visions and dreams during a period of about twenty-two years.

A dream and vision

At sundry times and in divers manners God has revealed his mind to man. By angels (Luke 2:10; Dan. 9:21). By Urim and Thummim (Num. 2:21; Eze. 2:6). By mouth (Gen. 18:3; Ex. 33:9). By voice (Ex. 3:4, Matt. 3:17). By inspiration (2 Pet. 1:20— 2 Tim. 3:16) and by dreams and visions (Dan. 7:1) God has made known His will.

Behold four great beasts

Daniel gives an outline history of the Gentile nations during the time God's ancient people are scattered among them in punishment for their perverse ways.

Nebuchadnezzar's colossus which was composed of precious metals was seen by Daniel as great ferocious beasts. Thus is set forth man's viewpoint compared to God's revelation. These beasts represent the moral character of the four kingdoms as seen by Nebuchadnezzar. They are shown to act without conscience, reason or moral responsibility before God. The characteristic features of Gentile dominion are clearly outlined by Daniel. Its idolatry, pride and degradation is set forth in Nebuchadnezzar. Its impurity, impiety and licentiousness is pictured in Belshazzar's wild revelry. Its daring blasphemy is shown in the decree of Darius who forbade prayer to be offered to any other being than himself.

Four Great Beasts

(1) The *Superiority* of Nebuchadnezzar is seen in the fact he was likened unto a *lion*. The *rapidity* and unabated strength of his conquests is shown in that the lion had *eagles'*

wings. In due time his conquests ceased and the old king slowed up, for his wings were plucked.

(2) Cyrus and Darius were likened to a bear which is less noble but perhaps more voracious and savage. The three ribs set forth the three kingdoms conquered by the Medes and Persians and which encouraged them to further conquests.

(3) Alexander the Great is symbolized by a leopard and he was indeed exceedingly fierce and suprisingly swift.

(4) The fourth Beast was the dreadful Iron Empire of Rome.

The four world empires are first represented as a mighty metallic colossus and second by four wild beasts. From man's viewpoint the present kingdoms of the world are the concentration of all material wealth, pomp and power. From God's viewpoint they are a set of wild, rapacious, bloodthirsty beasts devouring and destroying one another.

Beasts

The thin veneer of our civilization and boasted evolution has cracked in several parts of the world as well as in several sections of our own country. An ugly monster of mob rule has suddenly reared its head resulting in three lynchings in the last three days. Mobs more vicious than vipers and more bestial than beasts have killed in California, Maryland and Missouri and politicians are applauding the madness of the mob. Daniel saw worldly governments as beasts and current events prove the inspiration of the prophet. Consider Mussolini and Ethiopia together with the suicidal civil (Satanic) war in Spain.

I saw . . . I beheld . . . I considered (7:1-14)

Standing like a Cedar of Lebanon even in old age Daniel saw, beheld, considered and made known both the coming of the Anti-Christ and the coming again of the Christ of God. Two apocalypses are clearly made known. (1) The apocalypse of the Anti-Christ and (2) the apocalypse of Christ, the final conqueror and future King of Kings.

Four beasts came up from the sea

In symbolic prophecy waters generally denote peoples (Rev. 17:15), and winds the strife and commotion of war (Jer. 25:32) out of which rose the four great universal kingdoms, as already described in the prophecy of the second chapter. Here these kingdoms are symbolized by four beasts, as before in Chapter 2 by the four parts of the image. Earthly kingdoms are both human and bestial.

A fourth beast, dreadful and terrible

This verse is a perfect picture of the Roman Empire. It is history in advance of the events. It is interesting to study the different *histories* in the Bible.
   (1) The Ecclesiastical History of Israel in Lev. 23.
   (2) The Governmental History of Israel in Deut. 33.
   (3) The Jewish National History in Gen. 49.
   (4) Church History in Rev. 2 and 3.
   (5) Kingdom History in Matt. 13.
   (6) Gentile world History in Dan. 7.

Ten horns

These ten horns and also the little horn are yet to arise. After the rapture of the saints the world will be governed by ten kings or rulers. Out from these ten kings there shall arise the Anti-Christ who will assume full responsibility and who will finally declare himself the Dictator of the World. He will become the superman of the Evolutionists, a Pope, Mussolini, Hitler, Kaiser, Napoleon, Cæsar, Nero and Kemal Pasha all in one. (See "Riches from Revelation.")

Another little horn (7:8)

The Anti-Christ is to be revealed after the coming of Christ to catch away His Church. Immediately after the rapture, the world will be controlled by a league of nations composed of ten great rulers. Just about the middle of the Great Tribulation the Anti-Christ will declare himself as World Dictator. The minds of all mankind are now being prepared for just such a super-lord. God Almighty will be politely bowed out of His own world and man's day will culminate in hell let loose on earth. The expression "Another little horn" sets forth one more outstanding event yet to take place. Some of the most important events of the future will be

(1) The Rapture of the Church.
(2) The Great Tribulation.
(3) The Apocalypse of the Anti-Christ.
(4) The Coming of Christ to the Earth.
(5) All Israel saved.
(6) Satan confined in the bottomless pit.
(7) Christ's millennial reign.
(8) A new Heaven, New Earth and New City.

A comparison of this fourth beast with the *little horn* with *the man of sin* as portrayed by Paul in 2 Thess. 2 and *John's beast* (Rev. 13) proves beyond any reasonable doubt that they are all one and the same person, the last enemy of the Jews, the last dictator of the Gentile times, the Anti-Christ.

Three of the first horns plucked

The central figure of coming days will be the Anti-Christ. The outstanding, epochal event and personage of the age to come will be the apocalypse of the Anti-Christ. Slowly but surely he shall overcome all opposition. Three of the ten kings and kingdoms will be overthrown and after three and one-half years of subtle scheming, he will declare himself Dictator of the world and Hitler's past persecution of the Jews will be child's play compared to that of the Anti-Christ.

In this horn were eyes

"Eyes like the eyes of man," sets forth the wisdom, uncommon sense and sagacity of the coming superman. The world now awaits the coming of this knot disentangler, this super-Lloyd George, this master-Roosevelt, this Lenin-Stalin, Mussolini-Hitler iron man.

And a mouth speaking great things

The Anti-Christ will be noted for his wonderful eloquence. He will capture the imagination and attention of the world. He will be a Melanchthon, William Jennings Bryan and Gladstone all in one. He will become the world's boaster and blasphemer. Every little soap box prattler against God, the Bible, and Bible religion is a forerunner of the coming Anti-Christ. The blood curdling denunciation of God and Bible religion which have emanated from Russia and other places are all forerunners of the coming mouth speaking great things. It is astonishing to notice how the minds of men are being prepared before our very eyes for the Apocalypse of just such a personage as is described by Daniel in these inspired words. Anti-Christ will be Satan's masterpiece.

The ancient of days

"The ancient of days" in this verse refers to the eternal God and Father of our Lord Jesus Christ. His purity, wisdom and justice are set forth in verse nine which speaks of his garment being white as snow (purity) the hair of his head like pure wool (wisdom) his throne like the fiery flame (righteousness and justice) and his wheels as burning fire (beneficent providences).

"Thousand, thousands, ministered unto him"

What a scene that will be, when the holy, wise God of heaven sets up his righteous fiery throne, surrounded by the millions of bright shining angelic attendants. When that day dawns, as it certainly shall, I want to be on God's side.

One thousand thousand is a million. Thousand thousands however ministered unto him. These billions of holy, unfallen, spirit intelligences minister unto God, Christ and His saints.

Ten thousand times ten thousand stood before Him

Here are another 100,000,000 ministers standing at attention and awaiting orders. What a day of days the judgment

THE FOUR GREAT BEASTS / 99

day must be. Thus is represented the solemn assemblage of mankind awaiting their sentence from the supreme Judge. Each man, woman and child of Adam's race must give account to God. As a missionary the writer has often heard it said that the heathen will be a class among themselves and will be judged according to their light. The fact is, we shall each give an account of himself to God. Each individual is in a class by himself as each individual is a world in himself. Alone, we came into the world, and alone, we must depart, and alone, we shall stand before God to be judged. There is no such thing as mass salvation or mass judgment.

The ancient of days did sit

The future is as clear to God as the past is open to man's investigations. That which has been so minutely fulfilled assures us that all else shall be as minutely accomplished in God's good time and way. The Bible is a Divine record of Truth. It is absolutely reliable and in fullest accord with the known facts of 20th Century knowledge and discoveries. The first eleven chapters of the Bible cover a period of at least 2000 years, a third of human history and includes (1) The orderly series of creation from the lesser to the greater (2) The origin of the human family (3) The beginning of languages (4) The rise of nations (5) The fall of man (6) The universal flood and (7) The primeval creation, ruin and restoration of the earth. These and numerous other and equally interesting truths are recorded in the first eleven chapters of the first book of the Bible.

Every man made book of science needs revision as fuller knowledge is gained but the Mosaic account of creation has never been retouched and does not need retouching although written 3500 years ago.

His wheels as burning fire

Dominion and power in the earth and in the heavens is to be taken from Satan and beasts and transferred to Christ and His saints. All thrones in opposition to God and holiness are to be cast down and thrones in harmony with God and holiness are to be set up. The Ancient of Days shall ascend His throne of fiery, flaming justice and righteousness and his wheels (goings . . . conquests) shall be irresistible, all subduing and all conquering. The day of God and God's saints is yet to come.

The thrones were cast down

Satan is the prince (ruler) of the power of the air. (Eph. 2:2). He is at the head of a fully organized empire of darkness and evil. He not only has access to the earth—going up and down (north and south) and to and fro (east and west) in it but with his fallen angelic followers he also has access to the heavens and rules from his seat above the tree tops. He is not only the *god* of this age (2 Cor. 4:4) and the *prince* of this world (John 14:30) but he is also the *prince* of the power of the air or sky (Eph. 2:2). According to Rev. 12:7-10 God is to declare war on Satan and Michael the archangel is to give him battle and overcome him and cast him out of the heavens or sky above into the earth and thus the heavens shall be purified and made new. (See Riches from Revelation). The expression "the thrones were cast down" has thus a double significance (1) Satanic thrones or seats of power shall be cast down (2) thrones of Christ and his glorified saints shall be set up and there shall be a new Heaven (Rev. 21:1).

The thrones were cast down

The day is coming when all satanic seats of power and dominion both in the earth and in the heavens shall be overturned and swept away and God's saints shall be given dominion and sway. God's Israel shall yet be the head of the nations of earth and God's glorified saints of this church age shall be given dominion and power in the heavens. God's saints shall yet reign and rule. Israel, God's earthly saints shall reign over the earth while the glorified saints of this age shall rule in the heavens.

The judgment was set

Every living son and daughter of Adam's ruined race ought to be intensely interested in these stupendous events for they have each and all a case pending before the court of everlasting justice. There are several judgments mentioned in the Bible (1) Satan has been judged (2) Sin has been judged (3) The believers' sins have been judged (4) The believers' works will be judged *after* the *rapture* and *before* the *revelation* (5) The nations as nations will be judged by Christ just prior to the setting up of His Millennial Kingdom (6) The world including both Jews and Gentiles will be judged during the Great Tribulation and (7) The wicked dead shall be judged at the close of the Millennium when all the wicked shall stand before the great white throne. Daniel saw clear down to this judgment of the wicked dead. The judgments of God may seem painfully slow but they are absolutely sure and they grind exceeding small. It was as Paul reasoned of righteousness and judgment that Felix trembled (Acts 24:25). Secret sins (Rom. 2:6), idle words (Matt. 12:36), conduct (2 Cor. 5:10), desires and unbelief (John 3:18), shall all be dealt with when God judges mankind.

And the books were opened

How different the end of the world or age as made plain in God's word and as it is generally believed in the world today. World progress, prosperity, better times, the triumph of Christianity, the spread of Christian civilization, and the conversion of the world are great topics for a gullible public. How few realize that the whole colossus of man—the whole of man's day enterprise, inventions and greatness—is to crash and end in dust and ashes! Thrones are to be cast down, Christ is to sit on the Throne of the universes, judgment is coming, the crack of doom is about to be heard, the beast is to be burned, man's dominion is to pass and man, *boastful* man, *proud* man, *haughty* man, *high minded* man is to give an account of his deeds. The Books were opened.

The books were opened

The Old Testament scriptures will be there. (Book one.) Our attitude to God's truth as revealed in the Old Testament will be placed in the balances. The New Testament scriptures will be there. (Book two.) Our attitude to Christ's Word in the Gospels and to Paul's word in the Epistles and to John's word in the Revelation will all be placed upon the scales. The books of memory and conscience will also be there. (Books three and four.) Each act performed, every word spoken, together with every thought harbored in the mind will be weighed in the balances of eternal justice and holiness and a righteous verdict rendered. My God! What will poor sinners do? How about holiness fighters, Holy Ghost rejecters and Christ despisers THEN? The judgment was set and the books were opened.

The beast was slain

The little horn with eyes like the eyes of man had become a beast. His reign of terror, cruelty, and persecution of God's saints on the earth had run its course, his cup of iniquity was full, the time of judgment had come, and seized by the lion-lamb of the Tribe of Judah whose name he had blasphemed and whose followers he had slain, he is flung headlong into the lake of fire, his final and proper doom. Sin when it is finished bringeth forth death. Hell is always at the end of sin's road.

His body destroyed

The Anti-Christ is to be a real person with a real body. He is to control the whole antichristian system. He is to be the head, the climax and culmination of all sin, wickedness, deviltry and hellishness. He is to be a man. He is to be a man of sin. He is to be a superman. He is to be Satan incarnate, a complete counterfeit of Christ. He is to reign supreme over men for three and one-half years and then he is to be violently destroyed and his whole anti-christian-Babylon-system is to collapse and be swept for ever from the earth.

THE FOUR GREAT BEASTS / 103

And given to the burning flame

Anti-Christ will be flung with violence into the lake of fire. The lake of fire will be the final hell. He will be the first person to be cast into the burning flames of the future endless hell. Men and devils are endless beings. Sin, once committed can never be uncommitted and hence sin is endless. A lie once told can never be untold and hence becomes an endless lie. An endless lie told by an endless sinner merits endless punishment. Not until God is dead, will endless sin cease to merit endless punishment. There is no possible escape from the fact of an endless hell for endless, sinful men and devils.

The rest of the beasts

The ten kings are here described as beasts, i. e. senseless, quarrelsome, ferocious, selfish and unclean. The kingdoms and kings of earth may be considered by worldly Nebuchadnezzars as gold, silver and other precious metals, but as seen by God and his prophets they are beastly and must be finally destroyed.

One like the son of man

Daniel here sees the conquering Christ taking possession of the kingdoms of earth. He beholds the son of man and Saviour of sinners approach the everlasting Father and receive from Him dominion and glory and a kingdom.

Son of man

The expression "SON OF MAN" sets forth the Head of restored humanity. "SON OF DAVID" sets forth his royalty, "SON OF GOD" his deity and "SON OF MAN" his headship of humanity. The seed of the woman shall not only destroy Satan, but shall crush the Anti-Christ, the seed of Satan.

There was given him dominion

The population of the world is now 2,000,000,000 souls. This is an increase of about 20,000,000 a year for the past twenty years, a total increase in population of 400,000,000 for only twenty years. Asia alone has a population of 950,000,-000, Europe has 550,000,000, America has 130,000,000 and Africa 150,000,000. When one considers how difficult it is to keep peace even in one family or a small community or church, the problem of preserving the peace of the world becomes a problem of pyramidal proportions. Here is a job too big for the puny hands of man to handle. This mass of mankind is too big a job for even a Mussolini, Hitler, Roosevelt or the League of Nations. The situation now needs and loudly calls for one who is King of kings and Lord of lords. Such a one is coming and there is to be given Him dominion and glory and a kingdom.

There was given him a kingdom

Daniel foresaw and prophesied the coming of Christ with his saints in glory to rule the world. The mystery of Christ's Body, the Church, was not revealed to Daniel and hence the rapture of the Church was not seen by the Prophet. The secong coming of Christ FOR his saints is plainly taught in John 14:1-3; 1 Thes. 4:15-17; Acts 1:10-11; Heb. 9:28; Luke 17:34-35; Matt. 24:42; Matt. 25:13; 1 Thes. 5:5-7; 1 Cor. 15:51-52. Any theory that muffles the word "WATCH" is out of harmony with the teaching of the scriptures as to the second coming of Christ. After the rapture of the Church, the great Tribulation, the Apocalypse of the Anti-Christ and the destruction of Gentile World dominion, Christ shall take the kingdom and all people, nations and languages shall serve Him. Dan. 7:14 sets forth the Millennial kingdom of Christ.

An everlasting kingdom

The Millennial kingdom of Christ will end in a world wide rebellion led by Satan after his release out of prison for a little season. The rebellion will be ruthlessly stopped by the appearing of Christ, who, in flaming fire will destroy the wicked, fling Anti-Christ into the everlasting flames and the millennial reign of Christ will merge into the everlasting kingdom of Christ which shall enjoy perpetual increase and peace on the New Earth. The Millennial reign may cease but not the kingdom.

And all nations shall serve Him

A new monarchy is coming! A new head of humanity is near! The beast kingdoms and nations of earth have long written their histories in blood and tears. The long rule of sin and Satan has saturated the earth with blood and piled up the bones of the slaughtered sons of men. A new day is about to dawn and a new kingdom is about to come. In a universal, unending, righteous and peaceful kingdom Christ shall reign and all nations shall serve Him. Speed on, glad and glorious day.

I Daniel

How wilful, wayward and wicked, men must be to deny that Daniel wrote the book which bears his name. The heart of man is unquestionably deceitful and desperately wicked. Notwithstanding the fact that Christ Himself has set his seal on the book (Matt. 24:15) and that Daniel himself here declares his own authorship, the critics and infidels inside and outside of the Church still persist in their denunciations and denials. To what depths of stubbornness and stiff-neckedness may mankind sink when they will dare to put a lie on the lips of God, of Christ and His holy people. Daniel here declares that he was grieved. Daniel here says that the visions (not the histories) troubled him. Daniel here affirms that he received the truth directly from headquarters. Daniel here emphatically declares that not only the vision and dreams but also the interpretation of the things were all made known to him by revelation (Dan. 7:15-16). We cannot be Bible Christians and modernists, evolutionists, or higher critics.

My spirit in the midst of my body

The word body may also be translated *sheath*. Daniel regarded his spirit as altogether distinct from his body. As a sword in its *sheath* so was his spirit in his body. The tripartite nature of man is clearly revealed in the Bible. 1 Thess. 5:23 distinctly mentions spirit and soul and body. Heb. 4:12 "For the word of God is quick, and powerful, and sharper than any two edged sword, piercing even to the dividing asunder of soul and spirit, and of the joints and marrow, and is a discerner of the thoughts and intents of the heart." That there is a distinction and a difference between the soul and the spirit is here plainly revealed. The same distinction may be seen in the expression "My *soul* doth magnify the Lord, and my *spirit* doth rejoice in God my Saviour." Thus the threefold nature of man is clearly established. There can be no appeal from the clear statements of the inspired scriptures.

The visions of my head troubled me

Awed and dazzled by the remarkable revelations he was troubled because he understood not their meaning. Bent beneath the burden of these tremendous visions he was most anxious to know what they all meant.

The truth

Truth, not opinions, ideas, reasons, suppositions, assumptions. The writer once read Dean Farrar's "Eternal Hope" and he found on every page expressions such as "we may suppose" "we may assume" and "it is not unlikely." How different from "Thus saith the Lord." Between the covers of Darwin's "Origin of Species" which is headed for the Museums of the World, he *assumes* and *supposes* no less than 800 times. His ideas and conclusions he could not and knew he could not prove. That which was revealed to Daniel was *the truth*.

These great beasts

Nebuchadnezzar saw the imposing outward power and pomp of the times of the Gentile. Daniel, God's prophet, saw the true inward character of Gentile rule as rapacious and ruinous. It is remarkable that the heraldic insignia of the Gentile nations are mostly beasts or birds of prey. Even to this day we are reminded constantly of the power of the American Eagle, the British Lion, the Russian Bear, not to mention the yellow peril such as the Chinese Dragon. Selah!

These Great Beasts

(1) Beasts keep their own at any cost.
(2) They quarrel over that which rightfully belongs to another.
(3) Fly easily into a murderous rage.
(4) Kill for any coveted pleasure or possession.
(5) Are greedy; ruthless and bloodthirsty.

The kingdoms of earth are all bestial. Some day rule is to be transferred from beasts to saints.

The saints shall possess the kingdom

Daniel, a slave, is the representative of the nation of Israel in its servitude, solitude and sorrow. His insight into dreams and his wonderful wisdom sets forth the superiority of the people of God over their pagan overlords, while his exaltation to high office is a prophecy of the future glory of the people of Jehovah. "The saints shall possess the kingdom." Daniel's personal history was thus a type and prophecy of the future of his own people Israel.

Whose look was more stout than his fellows

The Anti-Christ will be a Mussolini, Hitler, Kemal Pasha, Lenin, Stalin, Kaiser, Napoleon and Pope all in one. It is striking and startling to notice that the Anti-Christ comes out of the ten kings who come out of the fourth monarchy. Not out of China, Japan, India, Africa, or the so called heathen world, but out of the so called Christian nations of the earth. These so called Christianized nations are represented by the prophet Daniel to be the most God dishonoring of all and climaxing their pride and blasphemy by producing the stout looking, wicked and wilful king, the Anti-Christ. The Bible thus reveals the *Christ* as *coming out of the East* and the *Anti-Christ* as *coming out of the West*. When Anti-Christ arrives he shall not substitute himself for Christ and act in

Christ's name as does the Pope. HE SHALL DENY CHRIST, OPPOSE CHRIST, AND EXALT HIMSELF ABOVE CHRIST.

The saints of the most high shall take the kingdom

The second coming of Christ is one grand event with two distinct parts. In the first part Christ is coming *for* His Saints and in the second part He is coming *with* His Saints. His coming is CERTAIN (John 14:1-3) PERSONAL (Acts 1:10-11) PRE-MILLENNIAL (Matt. 24:36) and VISIBLE (Rev. 1:7). Read Matt. 24:36-44 and Rev. 19:1-20, and also Rev. 20:1-10. That it does not refer to *death* is plainly seen from 1 Thes. 4:15-17, which declares that a portion of the human family shall never die. Death, therefore, cannot be the second coming of Christ. At the coming of Christ to the earth the saints shall receive and possess the kingdom. The Jewish Saints shall be the earthly people while the Church saints shall be the heavenly people during Christ's Millennial Reign.

See also Luke 17:34-35; 1 Thes. 5:2; Matt. 24:42; Matt. 25:13; 1 Thes. 5:5-7.

The horn made war with the saints

Full of hellish hatred against God and God's saints the Anti-Christ will make war against them. The persecution of the Jews by the German Chancellor and his government is child's play compared to the coming persecution by the Anti-Christ.

Think to change times and laws

All dictators think to, and, like Hitler and Mussolini do actually change times and laws. This change has to do not only with ordinary affairs of government but with religion and worship. The coming world Dictator or Anti-Christ will institute new modes of worship, impose new articles of faith, order and enjoin new rules of practice and enact, annul or reverse at pleasure, the laws both of God and man.

The horn made war with the saints, and prevailed . . .

This will be Satan's last attempt during the great Trbulation to destroy the Jewish race. There are today about 18,-000,000 Jews living in the world. Their very existence is a standing miracle and mystery. A race without a country, a people without a government, a nation without a home, hated, despised and persecuted, yet powerful, rich and indestructible. Submitting to neither assimilation, annihilation, nor elimination they are the miracle nation of the ages. Anti-Christ may war with them and prevail, but only *until* (7:21-22).

The saints of the most high shall take the kingdom

The saints mentioned here are the Jewish saints who shall become God's earthly ruling people during the millennium. The Church is a heavenly people whose eternal home is in the New City, New Jerusalem.

The saints possessed the kingdom

Wonderfully does this Old Testament prophetic book of Daniel and also the New Testament prophetic book of Revelation span the history of mankind from the creation of the world to the dawn of the world to come. The Book of Daniel gives the Alpha and Omega of all human history. The centuries have borne witness to the veracity of the Prophet and the Divine authorship of the Book which bears his noble name. Empires rise and fall exactly as foreseen and foretold. Flinging their colossal shadows across the pages of scripture we behold the giant forms of world empires on the way to oblivion.

Daniel clearly forecasts the march of history through the ages. Not only do we behold mankind moving across the stage of time and sense but we also see the mighty hand of living God ruling and over-ruling until at last His will is done in earth, as it is done in heaven, for "the saints" the meek, the lowly and the holy, "possess the kingdom for ever and ever." These are indeed and in truth precious pictures of a sinless world that open and close the blessed Book of God.

110 / DIAMONDS FROM DANIEL

Between the opening page of the Bible where we behold a sinless world (Gen. 1:1) and the closing page where we behold a new sinless world (Rev. 21:1-22-21) there is spread out the sad, painful panorama of six thousand years of sin, suffering, sorrow, sighing, conflict, warfare, turmoil and death. Nevertheless we are assured that "the saints," God's faithful few "shall possess the kingdom." (See "Riches from Revelation.")

Fear not little flock, the promises will be fulfilled. For the trusting and toiling, poor and suffering saints and servants of God, there is a good time coming. Possessing the divine nature and enjoying the divine inheritance they shall soon possess the divine kingdom.

He shall speak great words against the most high

Present events are rapidly paving the way for the coming "man of sin." STALIN OF RUSSIA speaking great swelling words against God! the Bible! and Religion! HITLER OF GERMANY hating and persecuting the Jews, who, while scattered, peeled and chastised are nevertheless God's people. MUSSOLINI OF ITALY willing to shake hands with and make a covenant with either God or the devil if either will prosper Italy. All modern dictators have some characteristics of the coming Anti-Christ who will be an atheist (Stalin) a hater and persecutor of the Jews (Hitler) and who will speak not only against God, but also against all things sacred and Divine (Lenin).

Think of a creature of earth speaking against the Creator of the Universe. A creature of a day criticizing the eternal Creator. Man is capable of terrible blasphemy. The coming Anti-Christ will speak marvelous things against God. His inferior predecessors have been and are many. The Pope of Rome is a blasphemer, for who can forgive sins but God alone?

Roman priests are likewise blasphemers for the forgiveness of sins is the prerogative of the Godhead. Public speakers both past and present have been and are guilty of the heinous sins of blasphemy. Mrs. W. M. Hack Congress-woman-at-large from the State of Illinois once declared "The next fifty years will see an end of all war. Women and mothers will accomplish that, and again, "It is they (the women and mothers) who will usher in the millennium."

Here is a twofold blasphemy which ascribes the work of God alone *to women*. If wars ever cease it will be *the Lord* who maketh wars to cease and not women (Psa. 46:9). When the millennium comes it will be the zeal of the Lord of hosts who will perform it and not woman. Who can bring in the millennium of peace and righteousness, but God alone? It looks to some of us that women may bring in a millennium, but it will be Satan's millennium. With their nudeness, haughtiness, stretched forth necks, wanton eyes, spiked heels, tinkling ornaments, chains, bracelets, earrings, headbands, rings, permanent waves that are not permanent, paint, poodle dogs, cigarettes and satanic brazenness and immodesty, it looks to some of us that, unless God steps in and cuts His work short in righteousness, the world is on the brink of irreparable ruin.

All dominions shall . . . obey Him

In his foreview of the future, Daniel beholds the Ancient of Days taking the kingdoms that all people, nations and languages should serve him. The prophet assures us that His kingdom shall be an everlasting kingdom and that all men shall serve and obey him. Sincere statesmen everywhere are agreed that the world today needs a superman who is able to grapple with and find a solution for the mighty intricate and international problems of the world. World problems are bigger than the brains of the greatest of earth statesmen and thinkers. The world is in need of some one with both wisdom and power. The world in fact is looking for him AND HE IS COMING. *CHRIST* who is both the *wisdom* of God and the *power* of God *is coming*. *After* man's day has run its course, *after* Monarchies have failed and democracies have gone to dust, after the Church age has run its course and the elect has been *called out*, after the Anti-Christ has done his worst THEN the Smiting Stone shall descend and fill the earth. Earth's rightful King, President and Dictator, shall ascend the throne and all dominions shall serve and obey Him. For such a Coming One all creation waits and groans, and to such a Coming One we say "Come, Lord Jesus."

Everlasting kingdom

The millennial reign and kingdom of Christ will merge into His Everlasting Dominion on the new Earth after the final doom of Satan and destruction of all the wicked.

The metallic man gives us the human view of world governments whereas the vision of them as fierce, devouring beasts sets forth the Divine view. Man thinks of the kingdoms of the world in terms of gold, silver, brass and iron whereas God views them as cruel, ferocious, wild, selfish, vicious beasts. Such government is to continue in some form down to the second coming of Christ. Not until Christ returns as King will the kingdoms of this world become the kingdoms of our Lord and of His Christ.

An everlasting God with his everlasting Christ is to set up an everlasting kingdom.

"THE SUM OF THE MATTERS"

The Vision of Daniel (Chap. 7)   The Four Beasts
Key

"These great beasts, which are four, are four kings."

The Vision 7:1-14	The Interpretation 7:15-28
"Four great beasts came up from the sea."	The sea represents the world of mankind while the four great beasts set forth the four great world empires of Babylon, Medo-Persia, Greece and Rome.
"The first was like a lion"	Nebuchadnezzar, majestic and mighty.
"And had eagle's wings"	Swift and powerful in conquests.
"The wings thereof were plucked"	Conquests were stopped.

THE FOUR GREAT BEASTS / 113

"It was lifted up from the earth"	Insanity of Nebuchadnezzar.
"Made stand—as a man"	Restoration of Nebuchadnezzar.
"A man's heart was given to it"	Reason returned and conscience awakened, Nebuchadnezzar lifted up his eyes to heaven and praised Jehovah.
"Another beast"	The Medes and Persians.
"Like to a bear"	Ponderous, powerful, cruel and avaricious.
"It raised up itself on one side"	Cyrus was higher than Darius.
"It had three ribs in the mouth of it"	Defeated and destroyed three kingdoms.
"They said thus unto it, Arise devour much flesh"	The victories of the past urged them on to greater conquests and worse cruelties. Success goaded them on to greater conquests.
"Lo, another like a leopard"	Alexander the Great, handsome, but cruel, stealthy and merciless.
"Four wings of a fowl"	Rapid conquests.
"Four heads"	The division of the empire under four generals after the death of Alexander.
"And dominion was given unto it"	World dominion of Alexander.
"Behold a fourth beast"	Rome.
"It devoured and brake in pieces"	Roman militarism.
"and stamped the residue with the feet of it"	Oppression and cruelty. What greed cruelty and rage is here foreseen by the prophet.
"It was diverse from all the beasts that were before it"	Rome crucified Peter, beheaded Paul, banished John, burned the Christians and butchered both men, women and children. Truly it was diverse from all the beasts that were before it. It is instructive to note the devolution from gold to mud and from the noble lion to the nondescript monstrosity.
"It had ten horns"	The ten horns correspond to the ten toes of the great and terrible image as seen by Nebuchadnezzar. These ten horns set forth ten kings

	which shall arise after the Church has been raptured and during the great tribulation and just before the Coming of Christ to reign as King of Kings.
"Another little horn"	The Anti-Christ, who shall make war with the Saints and prevail against them until Christ descends and destroys him.
"Before whom there were three of the first horns plucked up by the roots"	The Anti-Christ will brook no delay in his plans and no opposition to his policies. He forthwith destroys three of the ten kings who shall arise just previous to his own apocalypse.
"By the roots"	The merciless, murderous, ruthless activities of the Anti-Christ are thus foreseen and foretold.
"Eyes like the eyes of man"	The Anti-Christ is to be a human being with human sagacity and intelligence but charged, surcharged and controlled by Satan. The Anti-Christ will become an incarnation of Satan as Christ was God-incarnated.
"And a mouth speaking great things"	The Anti-Christ will be an egotist, boaster and blasphemer.
"I beheld till the thrones were cast down"	During the great tribulation, war shall be declared and waged against Satan and at that time the Satanic powers in the heavenlies will be cast down. See Rev. 12 and "Riches from Revelation."
"The Ancient of Days did sit"	The Everlasting Jehovah God.
"Whose garment was white as snow"	Purity.
"Hair of his head like pure wool"	Wisdom.
"His throne was like the fiery flame"	Justice.
"His wheels as burning fire"	Providential judgment in righteousness.

"A fiery stream issued and came forth from before him"	Jehovah God is to have the last word.
"Thousand, thousands ministered unto him"	Millions of unfallen angelic spirit intelligences wait upon Jehovah.
"The Judgment was set"	The Great White Throne Judgment of Almighty God.
"The books were opened"	(1) Memory (2) Conscience (3) Old Testament (4) New Testament (5) A movie-talkie-panoramic-picture of one's whole like. Selah!
"The beast was slain"	The blasphemous lips of the Anti-Christ are sealed in death.
"His body destroyed"	Just previous to the setting up of the millennial kingdom of Christ, Anti-Christ will be arrested and cast into the lake of fire.
"As concerning the rest of the beasts"	The empires of man.
"Behold one like the Son of man"	Jehovah—Jesus!
"Came with the clouds of heaven"	The apocalypse of Christ WITH his saints is herein set forth.
"And there was given him dominion and glory"	Here is the universal, everlasting, kingdom of Christ, a kingdom which shall never be destroyed.
"The saints of the most high shall take the kingdom"	The meek shall thus inherit the earth and God's people Israel shall once more be the head of the nations.

THE VISION OF THE
RAM AND HE GOAT

8

THE VISION OF THE RAM AND HE GOAT

The Key

"The ram which thou sawest having two horns are the kings of Media and Persia and the rough goat is the king of Grecia" (8:20-21).

The Vision 8:1-19	The Interpretation 8:20-27
"Behold a ram which had two horns"	The Medo-Persian empire with Cyrus and Darius as the two kings
"The two horns were high"	Both Cyrus and Darius were great kings
"But one was higher than the other"	Cyrus was the greater of the two kings.
"And the higher came up last"	Darius took the kingdom on the death of Belshazzar but the power and prestige of Cyrus increased until he was supreme.
"I saw the ram pushing westward"	The conquest of Babylon (westward) by the Medes and Persians (Ram)
"And northward and southward"	West, north and south set forth the world wide ambitions of the Medes and Persians. He finally conquered and ruled the world
"So that no beasts might stand before him"	(1) From the Divine viewpoint, empires, kingdoms, nations are bestial. (2) No other king or kingdom could withstand the onslaughts of the Medes and Persians.
"Behold an he goat"	Greece
"And touched not the ground"	Rapidity of Conquest
"The goat had a notable horn between his eyes"	Alexander the Great
"And he came to the ram"	War against the Medes and Persians
"And he was moved with choler against him"	The anger, fury, rage, madness of Alexander against the Medes and Persians.

"And smote the ram"	Victory of Greece
"And brake his two horns"	Defeated and destroyed the power of Cyrus and Darius
"There was no power in the ram to stand before him"	The collapse of the Medo-Persian empire before the onslaughts of Alexander
"Therefore the he goat waxed very great"	World wide conquests, victories and dominion of Alexander the Great
"And when he was strong"	When the empire of Greece was supreme
"The great horn was broken"	Death of Alexander 323 B.C.
"And for it came up four notable ones"	Division of the world empire of Greece under four Generals
"And out of one of them"	Out from one of the four rulers of the divided empire
"Came forth a little horn"	Antiochus Epiphanes, one of the outstanding types and fore-runners of the final Anti-Christ
"Which waxed exceeding great"	Antiochus Epiphanes became popular and powerful
"Toward the South and toward the East"	Egypt and Chaldea
"And toward the pleasant land"	Palestine
"And it waxed great even to the host of heaven"	Opposition of Antiochus toward the Jews, God's ancient people
"And it cast down some of the host to the ground"	Indignities, insults and humiliations to which the Jews were subjected by Antiochus Ephiphanes
"And of the stars to the ground"	The priests and leaders also were persecuted and humiliated by Antiochus Epiphanes
"Yea, he magnified himself even to the prince of the host"	The High Priest even was not exempt. Antiochus Epiphanes would brook no superior either in politics, parliament or even in religion. These are all striking characteristics of the future Anti-Christ
"By him the daily sacrifice was taken away"	Jewish worship was prohibited
"And the place of his sanctuary was cast down"	The temple was polluted and profaned by the wicked and fierce Antiochus Epiphanes. This king of fierce countenance, indwelt and con-

"And an host was given him against the daily sacrifice by reason of transgression. (Read 12-25)

trolled by Satan, attempted the wholesale destruction of God's holy people. He trampled upon the Old Testament scriptures and refused the Jewish people either the right or the privilege of temple worship. The expression "By reason of transgression" expresses the tragedy of it all. The sufferings of the Jews both past and present have been brought about because of their waywardness, wilfulness and wickedness. It was a punishment for national sins. The fact that Antiochus Epiphanes practiced and prospered was because of the perpetual perverseness of the people of God. This punishment for past and present national sins would continue 2300 days. This tribulation through which the Jews passed was a type and foreshadowing of the coming GREAT TRIBULATION as Antiochus Epiphanes was a type of the Anti-Christ. It is instructive to remember that the prophetic office seems always to be conected with the failure of God's people.

I will make thee know

"And I heard a man's voice between the banks of Ulai, which called, and said, Gabriel, make this man to understand the vision. So he came near where I stood; and when he came I was afraid, and fell upon my face: but he said unto me, Understand, O son of man: for at the time of the end shall be the vision. Now as he was speaking with me, I was in a deep sleep on my face toward the ground: but he touched me, and set me upright. And he said, Behold, *I will make thee know* what shall be the last end of the indignation for at the time appointed the end shall be" (Dan. 8:16-19).

With the eighth chapter of Daniel the book continues in the Hebrew language. The visions relate largely to the Jews and Jerusalem. The scene narrows from world wide prophecies to those affecting the covenant people of God.

The eighth chapter of Daniel depicts the Gentile powers as cruel, fierce, brutal, rapacious, wild beasts. We here look into the heart of world governments and see them as they really are and not as they apear to be. The whole genius of worldly government is seen to be selfish and cruel. Greed is shown to be Governor and Mammon is revealed as the Monarch. That which man calls "patriotism" and "commercialism" is seen and revealed by the spirit of God as animalism and diabolism. Dan. 7 and 8 gives us God's own viewpoint of the "powers that be." Gentile governments, sovereigns and rulers are revealed as wild, rapacious, unclean beasts that are destined to perish.

Westward . . . northward . . . southward

Eastward is not mentioned because the Persians came from the East and pushed on to the conquest of the world.

The goat had a notable horn

Alexander the Great was born 356 B.C. Daniel saw him and gave a succinct record of his rise and fall more than a century before he was born. The Ram actually became the emblem of the Medo-Persian empire as the goat was the emblem of the Grecian empire. The word ÆGEAN (sea) actually means Goat Sea. The son of Alexander was named AGUS which means "Son of the Goat."

And touched not the ground

Alexander conquered the world. The incredible swiftness of his conquests and victories is beautifully set forth in the expression "he touched not the ground." Meeting with little or no opposition, so fast and so furious did he advance that he became a world conqueror and world dictator when as yet a young man. The name of this "notable horn" still lives in history as ALEXANDER THE GREAT. Breaking the "two horns" of the Medo-Persians he became absolute master of the Persian Empire and the third world ruler of history.

Four notable ones

Alexander conquered Egypt, Palestine, Phœnicia and Tyre and ruled from Greece to the Ganges. Having conquered the world, but failing to conquer himself he died in India of intemperance, and left no successor. His kingdom was divided and fell to four of his generals.

The pleasant land

The different names given to the land of Palestine are (1) Canaan, Lev. 14:34, (2) The Holy Land, Zech. 2:12, (3) The Lord's Land, Hosea 9:3, (4) Emmanuel's Land, Isa. 8:8, (5) Land of Israel, 1 Sam. 13:19, (6) Land of the Hebrews, Gen. 40:15, (7) Land of Judah, Isa. 26:1, (8) Land of Promise, Heb. 11:9, (9) The Pleasant Land, Dan. 8:9 and (10) Palestine. It has been *THE NERVE CENTRE of the earth* since the days of Abraham. It has been THE TRUTH CENTRE from which has flowed a stream of Divine Revelation since the birth of Christ; and the STORM CENTRE of warring nations since the days of Joshua. It is to become THE PEACE CENTRE of the earth during the millennial reign of Christ and THE HOME CENTRE of all Israel throughout the ages to come.

The host of heaven

This host refers to God's people or the Jews and was fulfilled during the days of the Maccabees (Read V. 24). The Hebrews were God's holy and chosen people. They are cast off for the present, but shall be grafted in again after the rapture of the Church.

The prince of the host

This prince refers to the High Priest and points to Christ as may clearly be seen by reading V. 25. The little horn of Dan. 8:9 refers to Antiochus Epiphanes who waxed exceeding great, destroyed wonderfully, slaughtered the Jews, profaned holy things and actually challenged God to do battle against him. Antiochus was a John Baptist of the Anti-Christ.

That certain saint

It is more than likely that MOSES the representative of the law and ELIJAH, the representative of the prophets shall be permitted to take an active part in all the affairs of the Hebrew people. Daniel does not give the names of these two saints just as John the Revelator fails to give the names of the two witnesses of the Book of Revelation. Daniel saw that one was speaking and that the other was addressing the numberer of secrets or the wonderful numberer which would lead to the conclusion that one special angel has charge of numbers, as well as TIMES AND SEASONS which have to do with the Israel of God.

Unto 2300 days

The eighth chapter of Daniel describes the prophet's vision of a ram (Persia) with two horns (Cyrus and Darius) pushing its irresistible way to world dominion. The prophet then beholds an he goat (Greece) and notices that the goat has a special horn between its eyes (Alexander). In his hour of greatest triumph Alexander died and his kingdom was divided between four of his generals. One of these generals ruled over Syria. Out from the Syrian division of the Grecian empire the little horn (Antiochus the madman) came. Antiochus Epiphanes became the bitterest enemy of God's people. He entered the pleasant land (Palestine) persecuted the Jews, took away the daily sacrifice, polluted the temple, spilled the blood of swine upon the altar dedicated to Jehovah, killed 100,000 Jews, desolated the land, practiced and prospered. All this was foreseen and foretold by Daniel the prophet. Such desolation, destruction and devastation was to continue for 2300 days or six years, four months and twenty days or almost seven years. Antiochus Epiphanes was a striking type of the coming desolator, the Anti-Christ.

Here was a plain prophecy that Antiochus would not only forbid the Jews the right of free worship, but that the persecution would last almost seven years. The fulfillment of this prophecy may be read in Jewish history between the close of the Old Testament by Malachi and the opening of the New Testament by Matthew. It *was* prophecy. It *is* now history.

2300 days

These days are literally EVENINGS AND MORNINGS. For almost SEVEN years Antiochus stopped the Jewish worship forbidding them to offer their daily sacrifices. It points forward to the seven years of great tribulation.

Then shall the sanctuary be cleansed

How wonderful beyond words to describe that Daniel should have seen all these things for centuries before they became actual history. Long before Antiochus was born Daniel foretold what he would do. Daniel also foretold his doom and then beheld God's sanctuary cleansed. Antiochus may come to his end, but God's sanctuary endures. Cain may destroy his brother, but God will bring in His substitute, Seth, and through the line of Seth Christ the seed of the woman shall be born. Pharaoh may decide on the destruction of all baby boys, but God will save his Moses and give him an education at Pharaoh's expense. Saul may determine the death of David but God watches over his own and David is crowned king of all Israel. Antiochus Epiphanes may desolate the land, pollute the temple and profane God's holy things, but after Antiochus Epiphanes is dead, doomed and damned THEN shall the sanctuary be cleansed. God's word, God's people, and God's Sanctuary shall continue despite all the devils and madmen of either the past, present or future. It makes us shouting happy to know that GOD IS TO HAVE THE LAST WORD. Hallelujah!

Make this man to understand

Divine wisdom cometh from above. We may obtain a general knowledge in the schools of earth but wisdom and understanding concerning Divine things whether past, present or future cometh from above. It was the pleasure of Jehovah to make Daniel understand the vision.

Make this man to understand the vision

The critics of the book of Daniel alter the words THE VISION and in their place insert the words THE HISTORY. They seem to hate Daniel much more than they hate the devil. If they exercised their ingenuity in order to get rid of sin and Satan as they certainly do to get rid of these scriptures there would be fewer devils and more Daniels in our poor heart broken world.

At the time of the end shall be the vision

There is a definite day appointed by God for the full accomplishment of all these visions. It seems clear that these visions were not given in order to inform Daniel about Maccabean times merely but to reveal the truth about the Anti-Christ and the end of time.

It seems perfectly plain that while the little horn was to come out of the divided Grecian empire and that the prophecy received its partial fulfillment in the history of Antiochus Epiphanes and the terrible persecution of the Jews under his murderous regime, nevertheless, the prophecy was intended also as a profile picture of the future Anti-Christ and end time.

As Abel, Isaac, Joseph, Moses, Aaron and Melchizedek were types of Christ, (See "Gems from Genesis") so Antiochus Epiphanes was a type of the Anti-Christ and hence Daniel 8 is to have a future and fuller fulfillment.

"At the time of the end shall be the vision."

"I will make thee know what shall be in the last end of the indignation."

"At the time appointed the end shall be."

The above words of Daniel 8:16-19 give the key which unlocks this portion of Daniel's great vision. As the day of

Pentecost was but a partial fulfillment of the great prophecy of Joel, so Daniel 8:16-19 looks past Antiochus Epiphanes and Maccabean times to the Anti-Christ and the great tribulation.

The time of the end

The time of the end takes in the whole period from the close of the Old Testament Scripture to the reign of Christ over the Earth. The Church period under which we now live and which has already been running its course for 1900 years was not revealed by Daniel. When Christ was born he was born the King of the Jews. He was God's king and the Messiah of Israel. Rejected as King (which of course was all foreseen and foretold by God) He became, through death, the Savior of the World.

The last end of the indignation

The indignation or tribulation through which the people of God passed during the persecution under Antiochus Epiphanes was a foreshadowing of the greater indignation and tribulation of coming days after the rapture of the Church.

At the time appointed the end shall be

Known unto God are all his works from the beginning. The plans and purposes of God may be hindered, but cannot be finally frustrated. God's purposes for the world shall all be perfectly accomplished. God must win and they who side with God shall win with Him.

Daniel 8:17-19 while primarily dealing with Antiochus Epiphanes nevertheless sweeps on to the time of the end. Antiochus Epiphanes was simply a forerunner of the coming Anti-Christ. As Isaac and Joseph and Daniel were types of Christ so Cain, Nimrod and Antiochus Epiphanes were types of the Anti-Christ.

Greece with all its refinement, culture and art, produced the Old Testament Anti-Christ while the so called Christian nations produce the New Testament Anti-Christ. Antiochus

Epiphanes was the first great world ruler to systematically oppose the worship of the Jewish people and hence the need of prophecy in order to warn the godly and faithful remnant of his coming. Antiochus was the forerunner of the Anti-Christ. Had the plans and purposes of Antiochus succeeded the first advent of Christ would have been impossible and hence he stood in the same relation to the first advent of Christ that Anti-Christ does to His second advent.

The last end of the indignation

This is a very peculiar and very striking sentence. Unless clearly understood the book of Daniel in part will remain an enigma. There are two things to be noted (1) the indignation (2) the last end of the indignation. The indignation refers to God's punishment of His people, Israel, because of their perpetual disobedience. It sets forth the tribulation through which Israel and Judah would be pruned, purged and purified or otherwise perish in their perversity and sin. Such indignation began in the days of Nebuchadnezzar, was continued by Antiochus Epiphanes the Syrian, and later by Titus the Roman who in A.D. 70 murdered and massacred the people of God and scattered them to the so called four corners of the earth. The *indignation* continues until today and shall continue until this present Church Age has run its course. After the coming of Christ and consequent rapture of the Church the indignation will break out with added fury and for seven years hell will be let loose on the earth (Rev. 4-19). Toward the middle of this seven years of hell on earth Satan will be cast out of the heavens and cast down to the Earth (Rev. 12). The Anti-Christ will arise (typified by Antiochus) speedily followed by the false prophet and then, woe to the inhabiters of the earth for the devil is come down to you having great wrath.

The *indignation*, then, began with Nebuchadnezzar and continues to this hour. The *last end* of the indignation began with Antiochus Epiphanes and is yet to gather increasing momentum, force and fury until it reaches its consummation in the apocalypse of the Anti-Christ the coming satanic superman.

The king of Greece

No human ingenuity could have hit upon the interpretation of these divinely given dreams. Chapter 2:38 makes it perfectly plain that the head of gold was Babylon. Chapter 8:20 shows that the Medo Persian empire was to succeed that of Babylon while Chapter 8:21 gives us to understand that Greece was to follow Persia and that Alexander the Great was the great horn seen by the Prophet. Thus scripture is its own best commentary. Persia was the cruel bear, the animal which kills for the sake of killing and which tears for the sake of tearing, a heavy, cruel ponderous-beast-empire. The leopard or panther with its four wings wonderfully portrays the rapid triumphs of Alexander's armies and his insatiable love of conquest. The rough he goat was the Grecian empire and the great horn was its first king. Human sagacity alone can neither see nor foretell such stupendous events. This is the finger of God.

The rough goat is the king of Grecia

The Bible is self-explanatory. All light must be sought for and found in the Book itself. It may not always harmonize with our puny preconceived ideas but in that case we will change our ideas. Here is a clear prophecy which reveals that Greece would eventually gain imperial ascendancy and world wide supremacy. The rough goat like the abdomen of brass in the image of Nebuchadnezzar plainly sets forth the rise, progress and ruin of the third world empire of Greece. In the first image Greece was likened unto a leopard and here the first king of Greece is symbolized by a goat, yea, a *rough* goat.

Daniel beheld the rise and ruin of Alexander the Great long before the goat was born. Selah.

The latter time of their kingdom

The word THEIR has to do with the successors of Alexander the Great. The word KINGDOM refers to the kingdom of Greece which was divided after the death of Alexander.

When the transgressors are come to the full

There is a ripening of both sin and holiness. When the cup of Pharaoh's iniquity was full the judgment of God mercilessly fell. Both in time and in eternity men must increase either in goodness or wickedness either in sin or holiness so that the sinner shall become more and more and more sinful while the saint shall become more and more and more holy. Both in heaven and in hell there will be eternal increase. "He that is holy let him be holy still more and more and he that is filthy let him be filthy still more and more and more." Increase, development and growth is God's unalterable law. The lost shall become more and more like the devil while the redeemed shall become more and more like Christ.

A king of fierce countenance

Here is one principle of Biblical Hermeneutics or interpretation which materially helps in the understanding of many otherwise difficult portions of Scripture. It is the principle of the two in one or sometimes three in one pictures of persons, places and things.

Adam before the fall was in many ways a picture of the second man and last Adam, our Lord Jesus Christ. Holy, harmless, sinless, undefiled, monarch of all creation and ruling over a sinless world he plainly pictures Christ as the coming King.

Eve also before the fall was clearly a picture of the Bride of Christ. Taken from the wounded side of Adam, builded by God into a loving, winsome bride and helpmeet, reigning and ruling side by side over a sinless creation and with the whole world under their holy feet and obedient to their sovereign sway, Eve was plainly intended by Jehovah as a picture of the Bride of Christ.

The same thing applies to Abel, Noah, the Ark, Joseph, Moses, Melchizedek, Joshua, David, Solomon, Rebekah and Ruth, the Red Sea and Jordan, Egypt and Canaan. All alike were two in one pictures setting forth actual historical persons, places and events but also prophetic and typical of Christ and salvation from sin and the world.

The historical character in the eighth chapter of Daniel was also intended by the pen of inspiration to typify another madman, the coming Anti-Christ. It is one more two in one picture. Cain, Nimrod, Antiochus and Herod were each two in one pictures intended by the inspired penman to give a glimpse of the oncoming superman, the supreme blood rejecter, (Cain) city and civilization builder, (Nimrod) hater of God and enemy of God's people, (Antiochus) and would be destroyer of Christ, (Herod.)

A king of fierce countenance

The heart writes its contents on the countenance. Antiochus Epiphanes was to be an impudent, insolent, and vicious king. Fearing neither God nor man he was to be Satan's masterpiece of iniquity before the coming of the Anti-Christ of whom he was a striking shadow.

Understanding dark sentences

Master of the arts of deceit and diplomacy, versed in dark practices, wise to do evil and inspired by Satan, insincere and subtle he shall make dreadful havoc of both Jews and Gentiles who dare to cross his will and ways. Diplomacy is a high sounding word for deceit as so called Patriotism is often an excuse for plunder and wholesale murder. With serpentine subtlety, this fierce countenanced enemy of Christ and Israel, was to openly defy God and man, until his cup of wickedness overflows. Then he was to be broken without a hand of man being raised against him, for like Herod he was to be destroyed by God.

He . . . shall destroy the holy people (8:23-25)

Because of their transgression God's ancient people were given into the hands of Pharaoh who oppressed them 400 years. Despite the great deliverances wrought for them in Egypt and at the Red Sea they nevertheless forgot the Lord their God with the result that they were given into the hand of Chushan-rishathaim king of Mesopotamia who oppressed them eight years. Delivered again and again from their enemies by such warriors as Othniel, Ehud, Shamgar, Barak, Deborah, Gideon, Jephthah, Samson and David they nevertheless refused to profit by the sad experiences of the past. Their cup of iniquity filled, the indignation began by Nebuchadnezzar, was continued with increased force and fury by the Syrian madman Antiochus. A king of fierce countenance, Satan inspired and directed, by cruelty and craftiness he devastated the holy land and ruthlessly murdered the holy people who dared to disobey him.

The Holy People

The Jews were God's chosen, separated, elect people in Old Testament times. The God of the Bible is a holy God and it is impossible to conceive of a holy God being content with less than holiness in His people. "Holiness" is the key word of the book of Leviticus. God's people are commanded to be holy. By precept and promise God has urged holiness upon His followers. Holy men, moved by the Holy Ghost, penned the Holy Word of God which we call the Bible and we are assured that without holiness no man shall see the Lord. Heb. 12:14; Matt. 5:8; Matt. 5:48; Psa. 24:3-4; 1 Thes. 4:3; 1 Thes. 5:23-24; 1 Pet. 1:15-16.

Not by his own power

The perfidy of the priests, the treachery of the Jews, and the subtle power of Satan enabled Antiochus Epiphanes to prosper and practice and mightily destroy the people of God.

Filled with the devil the Syrian madman was to practice his cruelty and sacrilege in the Holy land, against God's holy sanctuary and chosen people. Peace and prosperity were to be two of his deceitful pass words and slogans thus foreshadowing the future Anti-Christ of the last days and end times. All cries of peace, peace when there is no peace and while the *prince of peace* is absent, are deceitful and damnable. Apart from Christ there is no peace for individuals or nations. The coming and power of Antiochus Epiphanes like the future coming of the Anti-Christ was after the working of Satan with all power and lying wonders and with all deceivableness of unrighteousness (2 Thess. 2:9-10). The dragon gave him his power (Rev. 13:2).

The prince of princes

These words look beyond the Jewish High Priest to the High Priest who is now on High and who is earth's rightful Prince, King, and Lord. Christ is the Prince of princes, King of kings and Lord of lords.

He shall be broken without hand

Antiochus Epiphanes conquered the south (Egypt) and then marched toward the pleasant land (Palestine). After humiliating the Jews he exalted himself even over the prince of the host (High Priest) took away the continual burnt offering (stopped Jewish worship) and profaned the temple. He set up heathen altars, sacrificed swines' flesh daily, and greatly oppressed God's people. His was broken without hand. The Hand of God was against him as it will be against the coming Anti-Christ.

I Daniel fainted and was sick

Here is proof positive if such were needed that sickness is not always the result of sin. Sickness may come from Satan as in the case of Job or as a judgment because of sin as in Ex. 15:26 or because of unworthy approach to the Lord's table as in 1 Cor. 11:30 or it may actually be produced as a superabundance of divine revelation and sympathy with the sorrow stricken saints of God. In Daniel we see a saint in such personal sympthy with the approaching sorrows of his own people because of their sins that he actually fainted and was sick certain days. He wept with those about to weep.

THE PROFOUNDEST PROPHECY
IN THE BIBLE

9

THE PROFOUNDEST PROPHECY IN THE BIBLE

I Daniel understood

The book of Daniel has been furiously fought and assidiously assailed by its foes. The attack on the book of Daniel began with Porphyry, a pagan, who was born in Syria A. D. 233. Modernistic preachers today continue the attack which was first launched by a pagan. THIS BOOK however CLAIMS TO HAVE BEEN WRITTEN BY DANIEL "I saw," "I Daniel, alone saw the vision," "I, Daniel, understood."

Ezekiel testifies to the existence and also the holy character of Daniel and no one doubts the genuineness of the book of Ezekiel (38:3). OUR BLESSED LORD set his seal to the whole book of Daniel and made it plain that his prophecy remained to be fulfilled more than 100 years after the death of Antiochus Epiphanes (Mtt. 24:15) RECENT ARCHEOLOGICAL DISCOVERIES have proved the genuineness of the book of Daniel and at the same time confused and condemned its too hasty critics. Not only so but the book as a whole, the prophecies, dreams and interpretations in particular, bear on their face the proof of divine inspiration. The paid flatterers and professional wise men of the Chaldean court never would have ventured to announce the utter destruction of Gentile governments and such a humiliating termination to Gentile supremacy. The book itself proves its own inspiration and authenticity.

I Daniel understood by books

Daniel was a student of prophecy. This fact ought to make us all ashamed of ourselves. WE REPEAT, Daniel was a student of prophecy. Daniel was a very busy man but he took time to study prophecy. Neither the devil nor the date setters disturbed or discouraged the diligent Daniel. He believed in prophecy. He believed in prophets. He believed in the study of prophecy. He believed in the study of the prophets. Daniel was a student of prophecy. Smart Alec's of both pulpit and pew who are either too lazy or too lopsided to study the prophecies, may sneer at sincere students of the scriptures and dub them as specialists, but such specialists find themselves in splendid company, for Daniel was a student of the prophetic scriptures. DANIEL UNDERSTOOD BY BOOKS. One of those books was the Book of Jeremiah. (Jer. 29:5-10) "Build ye houses, and dwell in them; and plant gardens, and eat the fruit of them; Take ye wives, and beget sons and daughters; and take wives for your sons, and give your daughters to husbands, that they may bear sons and daughters; that ye may be increased there, and not diminished. And seek the peace of the city whither I have caused you to be carried away captives, and pray unto the Lord for it; for in the peace thereof shall ye have peace. For thus saith the Lord of hosts, the God of Israel; Let not your prophets and your diviners, that be in the midst of you, deceive you, neither hearken to your dreams which ye cause to be dreamed. For they prophesy falsely unto you in my name: I have not sent them, saith the Lord. *For thus saith the Lord, That after seventy years* be accomplished at Babylon *I will visit you*, and perform my good word toward you, in causing you to return to this place." Thanks to the patient toil, prayerful study, and persistent efforts of Daniel much of what was a profound mystery is now made plain.

The Book of Daniel was written 600 years earlier than the Book of Revelation. They are nevertheless companion prophecies and must be studied together. Both great prophecies treat of the same great subjects and use almost exactly the same signs and symbols. Both deal in dates and hence are pre-eminently Jewish and both have what may be called a sacred arithmetic. The stupendous scenes and startling events of the end of the world are pictured and portrayed in both of these prophetic books. Thanks to the patient and prayerful toil and study by Daniel we repeat much of what was once profound mystery is now made plain. "I understood by books."

"AFTER SEVENTY YEARS I WILL VISIT YOU" is an unconditional promise. God promises to visit and restore His people Israel. On the all-sufficient basis of the Word of God in Jeremiah, Daniel made his request known unto God. Daniel's prayer and petition was made to God on the ground of God's Word, God's Righteousness and God's Justice.

I set my face to seek

"Ask and ye shall receive, seek and ye shall find." There is only one sure and safe way of Salvation! We must set our face to *seek* until we find. There is only one sure and safe way of sanctification. We must set our face to seek until we receive the mighty sin killing baptism with the Holy Ghost. There is only one sure and safe way of inspiration, and revelation! We must set our face to seek by earnest prayer and unceasing supplication. Any other way of salvation, sanctification or revelation is Satan's way. The kingdom of heaven is taken by *violence*. We must *agonize* to enter. We must set our faces resolutely toward the skies or we shall all land in hell.

To seek by prayer

Preachers and people alike today are pointing out an easy way which they call the way of faith. Saving faith, however, is impossible without prayer, Faith which saves the sinner and brings sanctification to the saint is preceded and always preceded by soul travail. All other faith is spurious. The modern cry of ONLY BELIEVE is a satanic delusion. To a sinner, saving faith is impossible apart from conviction, repentance and prayer. To a believer, sanctifying faith is an utter impossibility apart from consecration, hunger for holiness and earnest prayer. Divine truth is revealed to searchers. The secrets of God are given only to sincere seekers.

Prayer . . . and supplications

Daniel's life was crowded with critical concerns and events. His high and honorable place and position in the courts of

Babylon and Persia, his great responsibilities as a high servant of state, his pressing duties and problems to which he must constantly and promptly attend, nevertheless, hindered not his conscientious performance of his first duty and responsibility toward God, his own soul and the course of God's kingdom. He consistently and religiously sought first the kingdom of God and his righteousness (holiness). Prayer to him was not only a high and holy privilege, it was his first and biggest business. Thrice daily Daniel could be seen upon his knees in secret devotion and prevailing prayer. God's Book, the Old Testament was his constant companion and guide. The promises of God were a perennial source of praise and prayer. A busy man of his times in a busy capital of the world, he nevertheless repaired to his secret chamber of worship, devotion, prayer and fresh perusal of the promises and precepts of his God. He understood by books. He studied the Bible. He searched the prophecies as every devout follower of God and leader of men does. He discovered the truth of God's future dealings by a constant perusal of the prophecies and obtained marvelous revelations from God by a constant pleading of the promises of God's imperishable Word. He "understood by books."

Daniel sought by "prayer" (general request and desire) and "supplications" (pressing, pleading, prayer and entreaty) "with fasting" (self-denial in things legal, right and legitimate) "and sackcloth" (penitence and mourning) and "ashes" (humiliation and unworthiness). No wonder Daniel understood.

I set my face unto the Lord

With firmness of faith, fervor of affections, and fixedness of purpose, Daniel set his face to seek the Lord. He set the Lord before him and set himself as in the presence of God.

Prayer . . . supplication . . . fasting . . . confession

Moses made known to Israel that if and when they were in exile because of their sins, they should REPENT and

CONFESS, God would remember His Covenant and save them. Promise and prayer thus precede the blessings of God. Daniel takes the sins of Israel and makes them his own. He identifies himself with the sinful and erring nation of Israel. As their representative and priest he accepts the punishment due their iniquity, prays, supplicates, intercedes, fasts, and confesses. Daniel thus beautifully typifies Christ, the sin bearer and intercessor. The word "supplications" is in the plural.

Great and dreadful God

The dreadful God. "O Lord . . . the DREADFUL God." His greatness and dreadfulness had been declared by the Calamities which He had brought upon the nation of Israel. The DREADFULNESS of God was declared in the deluge which overtook the old world because of their sin. The DREADFULNESS of God was declared in the destruction of Sodom and Gomorrah, the cities of the plain, upon which God rained fire and brimstone.

When Lucifer, the son of the dawning, rebelled against His Creator in the Ages past "The Dreadful God" smote him with judgment and he became the black winged monster of death and destruction known now to us as Satan, the devil.

When Adam sinned "The Dreadful God" banished him from Eden and cursed the ground for man's sake.

When the Antediluvians refused to enter the only place of salvation and security provided for them the flood came and swept them from the earth. "The Dreadful God" opened the fountains of the great deep and let loose the judgment waters from above and destroyed the race saving only eight people alive.

When Pharaoh stuck his mailed fist in the face of Jehovah and refused liberty to the oppressed Hebrew people "The Dreadful God" wrapped a watery shroud around his body and today Pharaoh is a mummified corpse in a British museum while God moves forward to the fulfillment of all His gracious plans and purposes and the Hebrew race marches on to its prophesied place among the nations.

When the Canaanites refused the will and way of the Almighty and spurned the opportunity to amend their ways "The Dreadful God" turned the "hornets" loose upon them and finally swept them from the earth which groaned beneath their sin and shame.

When Saul turned a deaf ear to the warning voice of God's anointed Samuel "The Dreadful God" departed from him and answered him no more and he became the first suicide mentioned in the Bible and has been wailing in Sheol for 3000 years.

When Nebuchadnezzar allowed his heart to be lifted up with pride and refused to break off his sins by righteousness "The Dreadful God" withdrew His protecting Hand and the once mighty man became a mad monarch. Instead of feasting on grouse he ate grass until he discovered that Jehovah ruled in the kingdom of men.

When Belshazzar's cup was full, "The Dreadful God" wrote his doom on the wall beside the candlestick. Weighed in the balance and found wanting, "that night was Belshazzar the king of the Chaldees slain."

When Herod beheaded the Baptist he filled up his cup of iniquity, and "The Dreadful God" permitted an insignificant GERM to do its deadly work and Herod was eaten by worms and died.

When Ananias with his selfish wife Sapphira lied to Peter and the Holy Ghost, "The Dreadful God" let loose his thunderbolts of wrath and the hypocritical pair dropped dead in the meeting house.

When Babylon, Persia, Greece, Rome, Egypt, Nineveh and Jerusalem turned away from righteousness which alone exalteth a nation, "The Dreadful God" turned away from them and decay, dissolution and desolation and death inevitably followed and today we may ask, "Where is beautiful Babylon?" "Where is the glory that was once the heritage of Greece? Where is the regal splendor of Rome? And where is the joy that once reverberated over the hills of Jerusalem, the city of the Great King?"

Neither men nor nations can sin against "The Dreadful God" and escape the consequences of their self chosen ways.

We have sinned

The accumulated sins of the Jews were deeply felt by the prophet. To Daniel, the justice and righteousness of God had been vindicated in their past punishment and hence the cry for forgiveness and mercy. Daniel links himself with the chosen people, for God's people are one. *"Our* Father," "Give *us* this day," "Forgive *us*," "Lead *us* not into temptation," *"We* have sinned." This prayer of Daniel is a model of (1) Confession (2) Supplication (3) Intercession (4) Faith.

All Israel that are near and far off

Judah and Benjamin were NEAR for they were by the rivers of Babylon while the ten tribes were afar off in the land of Assyria.

For the Lord's sake

All New Testament truth is germinal in the scriptures of the Old Testament. Forgiveness, mercy and blessing has been, is now, and ever shall be conditional upon the merits of our Lord Jesus Christ. God's promises and blessings in the past, present and future are all fulfilled and bestowed in and for the sake of Christ. In the name of the Lord Jesus, we pray. For Christ's sake, we plead. Here is the key which unlocks the heavens.

For thy city and thy people

It is very touching to notice the expression throughout the Bible such as thy city and thy people. In speaking to the prophets over and over again God refers to the Jews as thy people and to Jerusalem as thy city as though He had rejected them because of their wicked ways. In the above passage

Daniel turns the tables and speaks to God of THY city and THY people. This play upon words is very interesting and instructive.

THY CITY and THY PEOPLE

The Hebrews were God's people. The land of Canaan was God's land. Jerusalem was God's city. Jehovah called the Hebrews "my people" and Jerusalem was the city of the Great King.

God's people, however, sinned against their gracious God and were disowned. In speaking to Daniel God refers to the Hebrews as thy people and in speaking to God Daniel refers to them as thy people. This is pathetic indeed but it is also one more proof of the Divine inspiration of the book of Daniel.

Whiles I was . . . confessing

"I acknowledged my sin . . . I will confess my transgressions," said David (Ps. 32:15). "If we confess (1 John 1:9) we may be forgiven and cleansed." "Whoso CONFESSETH AND FORSAKETH . . . shall obtain mercy" (Prov. 28:13). It was while Daniel was praying and confessing that Gabriel was caused to fly swiftly and give Daniel the greatest revelation ever vouchsafed to mortal man, i. e. the prophecy of the seventy weeks.

Whiles I was . . . speaking

Some of God's answers startle us with their swiftness and suddenness. Yea, even before we have called with our lips God has answered the previous cry of the heart.

The time of the evening oblation

Three o'clock in the afternoon was the time of the evening oblation. It was at this time so sacred to God and the people of God that the angel Gabriel came nigh to Daniel, talked with him and instructed him in the things of God and the future. At three o'clock in the afternoon Abel offered his lamb. At three o'clock in the afternoon Samuel was to offer the lamb. At three o'clock in the afternoon the passover lamb was slain.

At three o'clock in the afternoon the lamb was sacrificed and Jehoshaphat overcame his enemies and at three o'clock in the afternoon Christ the lamb of God bowed His head and died. It was the time of the evening oblation. The ways of God are equal and the works of God are right. On Thursday afternoon April 14th, 1900 years ago at three o'clock in the afternoon Christ the Son of God bowed His sacred head and died on the cruel cross. It was the time of the evening oblation.

Three o'clock in the afternoon, then, was THE TIME of the evening oblation. It was THE TIME when Moses offered the Paschal lamb. It was THE TIME that Samuel offered the lamb just before the war with the Philistines. It was because Saul offered the lamb BEFORE the time (thus also usurping the priests' office) that Samuel rebuked Saul. It was THE TIME that Jehoshaphat offered the lamb and which was the first step in his glorious victory. It was THE TIME that God's lamb was offered on the cruel cross of Calvary, the time of the evening sacrifice. How inerrant, complete, marvelous, wonderful and sublime is the word of God in both Old and New Testaments. It is more than likely that Daniel spent all the former part of the day in fasting, prayer and supplications. Whilst thus earnestly engaged God answered the exact hour and moment in which Christ died on Calvary.

Gabriel

Angels inhabit every part of God's universe. There are evil angels, (Eph. 6:12, Matt. 25:41, Rev. 9:11); good angels (Luke 9:26, Acts 10:22, Rev. 14:10); guardian angels (Matt. 18:10, Psa. 34:7); and chief angels, (Dan. 10:13, 9:21). Daniel's praying and confessing brought quick results. God sometimes surprises by the suddenness of His answers to our earnest heart cry. Gabriel was ordered to fly swiftly and answer the soul cry of the prophet.

Key:
   "Thy people." (Jews).
   "Thy city." (Jerusalem). Dan. 9:24-27.

The greatest prophecy in the Bible

Dan. 9:24-27 "Seventy weeks are determined upon thy people and upon thy holy city, to finish the transgression, and to make an end of sins, and to make reconciliation for iniquity, and to bring in everlasting righteousness, and to seal up the vision and prophecy, and to anoint the most Holy. Know therefore and understand, that from the going forth of the commandment to restore and to build Jerusalem unto Messiah the Prince shall be seven weeks and threescore and two weeks; the street shall be built again, and the wall even in troublous times. And after threescore and two weeks shall Messiah be cut off, but not for himself; and the people of the prince that shall come shall destroy the city and the sanctuary; and the end thereof shall be with a flood, and unto the end of the war desolations are determined. And he shall confirm the covenant with man for one week; and in the midst of the week he shall cause the sacrifice and the oblation to cease, and for the overspreading of abominations he shall make it desolate, even until the consummation, and that determined shall be poured upon the desolate."

Thy holy city

Jerusalem was first named Jebus. It was captured and fully occupied for David by Joab. It became the City of David—Zion—the City—and Jerusalem.

The ark of the Covenant was brought to Jerusalem, and thereafter it became the centre of Israel's worship. Its greatest glory was reached in the reign of Solomon. It has been besieged and laid in ruins more times than any other city in the world. It was destroyed by Nebuchadnezzar, rebuilt by Ezra, Zerubbabel and Nehemiah, and finally destroyed by Titus and the Romans.

During the great war of 1914-1918 it was captured by General Allenby and is now controlled largely by England, who is its caretaker and janitor.

Both Babylon and Jerusalem are to be rebuilt in the latter days only to be completely destroyed by the closing judgments of the Great Tribulation.

The commandment to restore and to build

The command to restore and to build was given to Nehemiah by Artaxerxes in the twentieth year of his reign. (Nehemiah 2:1-8). This date is therefore settled. Nehemiah occupied the high office of cup bearer to the king. This was a position of trust and brought Nehemiah into closest contact with the king. Nehemiah's journey up to Jerusalem was under a regular princely escort. After secretly reviewing the whole situation in Jerusalem Nehemiah decided *to build* (2:17). Nehemiah was at least 12 years away from the Persian court, superintending, establishing and governing Jerusalem.

Seventy weeks

Here is given one of the most comprehensive revelations ever given to man. The startling announcement is made that seventy sevens are determined upon Daniel's people to terminate their apostasy, end their sins, bring in everlasting righteousness and perfectly fulfill all vision and prophecy. The Holy Spirit plainly points out that after seventy sevens, or 490 years, Jerusalem will be rebuilt, Israel will be restored, all things fulfilled and Christ reign and rule without a rival. Dan. 9:24-27 unmistakably declares that in 490 Jewish years God would perform His whole work which He had promised and prophesied in all the scriptures.

Seventy weeks

The word WEEKS may also be translated SEVENS. Seventy SEVENS are determined upon thy people. Seventy weeks of years are determined upon thy holy city. Seventy sevens or 490 years are determined to finish the transgression and to make an end of sins. Daniel plainly declares that in 490 years all things would be accomplished, transgression would be finished, sins would be for ever ended and all prophecy fulfilled. In 490 years from the going forth of a certain commandment, everlasting righteousness would be brought in.

Seven Weeks: The seventy sevens are divided into three groups i. e. (1) seven weeks; (2) sixty-two weeks; (3) one week or (1) seven sevens or forty-nine years. (2) sixty-two sevens or 434 years and (3) one seven or seven years. Within the first group or forty-nine years Jerusalem was to be rebuilt. Within the 2nd group or 434 years the Messiah was to be cut off or crucified and then within the period of the last seven years the prince or Anti-Christ was to appear and be finally destroyed by Christ. The Church age or present dispensation of grace was not revealed by Daniel. Daniel stands on Jewish ground and the time from the crucifixion of Christ, to His second coming to catch away his Church and take unto Himself His bride, was not seen by Daniel. The past 1900 years of the Dispensation of the Holy Spirit was not given to the prophet Daniel and hence is not to be reckoned in the seventy sevens or 490 years. Within these WEEKS or SEVENS OF YEARS the chastisement of Israel must end and the nation be restored and established in everlasting righteousness within the borders of their own promised land. The SEVENTY SEVENS then were to be divided into (1) seven or 49 years; (2) sixty-two or 434 years and (3) one or seven years. In the seven weeks or 49 years Jerusalem was to be rebuilt. This was fulfilled as may be seen by reading Ezra and Nehemiah. In the sixty-two weeks or 434 years thereafter Christ was to come. Thus sixty-nine weeks or 483 years have already been fulfilled which leaves only one week or seven years of the great tribulation when Jehovah again will deal with the nation of Israel and which is yet future. The birth of the Church at Christ's resurrection, its baptism into one body at Pentecost, its 1900 years of history and the oncoming rapture was not seen by Daniel the prophet. Seventy periods of sevens was to include the whole troubled history of God's ancient people the Jews, and of the holy city Jerusalem. Sixty-nine heptads are already in the past while the seventieth is yet future. The interval was to be filled by the Church of which no revelation is here given. There is an unnoticed period of 1900 years during which time God is calling out from both Jews and Gentiles, a people for Himself (Acts 15).

To finish transgression

This refers to Israel's transgression. The rejection of Christ as Messiah was peculiarly Israel's transgression. At the close of the Great Tribulation, Israel shall receive Christ as their King, and thus the transgression shall be finished. It was not the Jews alone who rejected Christ. The whole world was involved in the crucifixion of God's son. The Hebrew race as a whole was represented by those who shouted "Away with Him, away with Him." Jews and Gentiles alike are held blood guilty of the murder of God's only begotten Son. In a peculiar sense however, the rejection of Christ was the climax and culmination of Israel's long continued transgressions.

Messiah the Prince

The word "Messiah" means "the anointed one" while the term "prince" means ruler, king. The expression "Messiah the Prince" refers to Christ as the Anointed King of the Jews. 483 Jewish years after the commandment to restore and to rebuild Jerusalem Christ offered Himself as the promised Messiah and Prince. The account is as follows:

"And when they drew nigh unto Jerusalem, and were come to Bethphage, unto the mount of Olives, then sent Jesus two disciples, Saying unto them, Go into the village over against you, and straightway ye shall find an ass tied, and a colt with her; loose them and bring them unto me. And if any man say ought unto you, ye shall say, The Lord hath need of them; and straightway he will send them. All this was done, that it might be fulfilled which was spoken by the prophet, saying, Tell ye the daughter of Sion, Behold, thy King cometh unto thee, meek, and sitting upon an ass, and a colt the foal of an ass. And the disciples went, and did as Jesus commanded them, and brought the ass, and the colt, and put on them their clothes, and they set him thereon.

"And a very great multitude spread their garments in the way; others cut down branches from the trees, and strewed them in the way. And the multitudes that went before, and they that followed cried, saying, Hosanna to the son of David; Blessed is he that cometh in the name of the Lord; Hosanna in the highest. And when he was come into Jerusalem, all the city was moved, saying, Who is this? And the multitude said, This is Jesus the prophet of Nazareth of Galilee."

Four days later Christ was crucified. Cut off, but not for himself. He arose three days later and ushered in the present church age which shall continue until He returns to rapture His church. Seven years after the rapture of the Church, *Messiah the Prince* shall descend to the earth with His saints, set up His millennial kingdom and reign as king of kings and Lord of lords. Thus will be fulfilled the great prophecy of 490 years.

To make an end of sins:

The sins are particularly the sins of Israel and Jerusalem. We need to remember that Daniel's people and their holy city are in view in this prophecy.

Isa. 59:20 "And the Redeemer shall come to Zion, unto them that turn from transgression in Jacob, saith the Lord."

Isa. 27:9 "By this therefore shall the iniquity of Jacob be purged; and this is all the fruit to take away his sin; when he maketh all the stones of the altar as chalkstones that are beaten in sunder, the groves and images shall not stand up."

Rom. 11:26-27 "And so all Israel shall be saved: as it is written, There shall come out of Sion the Deliverer, and shall turn away ungodliness from Jacob: For this is my covenant unto them, when I shall take away their sins."

To make reconciliation:

Israel shall recognize and accept Christ as their long promised and expected King. Their sins of rejection, unbelief and rebellion shall end, Judah shall be reconciled to Israel and Israel shall be reconciled to Judah and both shall be reconciled to Christ and their terrible iniquity shall be purged away.

Zech. 13:1 "In that day there shall be a fountain opened to the house of David and to the inhabitants of Jerusalem for sin and for uncleanness."

To bring in everlasting righteousness

This sweeps beyond the birth and death of Christ, beyond his resurrection and ascension, down the centuries which compose the present Church age, past the great tribulation and millennium and on to the New Heavens and New Earth when everlasting righteousness shall be brought in. Not until after the resurrection and judgment of the wicked dead will everlasting righteousness be an accomplished fact.

This will include the conversion, cleansing, redemption and restoration of Israel. God will put his law in their hearts and He alone will be their God and they shall be his people. Israel shall love and serve God and His Christ, and righteousness shall fill the earth.

To seal up vision and prophecy

The failure and disobedience of God's ancient people brought in the order of ministers known as prophets. God personally dealt with Adam, Cain, Abraham, Isaac, Jacob and Israel. It was not until Israel demanded a king and the nation became stiff-necked and rebellious that Jehovah ordained prophets to call the nation back to the ways of truth and righteousness. The presence of prophets in Old Testament times was always proof of the perverseness of God's people. But for the failure and disobedience of God's people there had been neither prophets nor seers. With transgression finished, sins ended, iniquity purged, reconciliation accomplished and everlasting righteousness brought in, there will no longer be needed either prophets or SEERS and hence, like the ceremonial law of Moses they will be done away. 1 Cor. 13:8-10 "Charity never faileth: but whether there be prophecies, they shall fail: whether there be tongues, they shall cease; whether there be knowledge, it shall vanish away. For we know in part, and we prophesy in part. But when that which is perfect is come, then that which is in part shall be done away."

Even in troublous times

How troublous, is told in the graphic words of Nehemiah, 4:16 "And it came to pass that the half of my servants wrought in the work, and the other half of them held both the spears, the shields, and the bows, and the habergeons; and the rulers were behind all the house of Judah" 4:21 . . . "So we laboured in the work: and half of them held the spears from the rising of the morning till the stars appeared."

Unto the Messiah the Prince

From the going forth of the commandment to restore and rebuild Jerusalem unto the day when Christ entered Jerusalem on Palm Sunday was exactly 483 years.

Biblical students are now generally agreed that this is one of the most undeniable prophecies of Christ. The coming and kingdom of Christ is the golden key which unlocks this profound inspired prophecy. It is universally allowed that the seventy weeks mean seventy sevens of years or 490 years. The Jews have proved themselves guilty of the most obstinate unbelief, first by rejecting Christ, and second by expecting another Messiah so many centuries after the time fixed for his coming and after the now acknowledged fulfillment of the other parts of the same prophecy. Blinded by unbelief they stagger forward to the apocalypse of the Anti-Christ who shall come in his own name and whom they will accept.

But not for himself:

Born in another man's stable, cradled in another man's manger with nowhere to lay his head during his life on earth, and buried in another man's tomb after dying on a cursed cross, the Christ of God and Friend of the friendless was indeed cut off and had nothing (see margin).

150 / DIAMONDS FROM DANIEL

Desolations are determined

What a profound prophetic picture of all Jewish history is thus set forth. "Desolations are determined." There is not a people anywhere on earth who have gone through the desolations through which the poor persecuted Jew has gone. There has never been peace in Jerusalem for the Jews since Daniel uttered this stupendous prophecy and passed to his rest and promised reward. For 2500 years this scripture has been fulfilled before the eyes of an unbelieving world. In three words God predicted the history of the Jews for more than twenty-five centuries. "Desolations are determined." This has been and is being marvelously verified. Neither Zionist movements nor world protests can stop the exact minute fulfillment of the scripture of truth. God foresaw, foreknew and foretold, that for the disobedient Jews "desolations were determined." The Jews of America may hold their protest meetings, Jews of England may stir up the British parliament, Zionist conventions may pass resolutions BUT "desolations are determined." The boastful cry of the Jews "His blood be upon us and our children" only increased the determined desolations. Not until Israel and Judah repent and turn to Jehovah, and cry mightily to Him for help shall the determined desolations cease. There is only one way to stop the judgments of God and that is to stop the sin which brings the judgment.

The Prince that shall come

All prophecy has a near and a distant fulfillment. The prince that shall come refers (1) to Titus the Roman Prince who not only destroyed the city and the sanctuary, but ploughed up the ground, murdering and plundering on every hand. (2) To the Anti-Christ, the prince who is yet to come, and who shall destroy the city and the sanctuary.

He shall confirm the covenant . . . for one week

After the rapture of the saints, the Anti-Christ is to make an agreement with the Jews for one week of sevens or seven years. In the middle of the week or after three and one half years his covenant is to become a "scrap of paper." He breaks his covenant and hell is let loose on earth.

Until the consummation

Verse 27 contains a brief biography of the Anti-Christ in which we see (1) His coming (2) His work and (3) His doom.

Verses 24-27 contain everything in seed from Daniel's day to the restoration of all things in the New Heavens and the New Earth. These verses are clear that (1) Christ shall be triumphant (2) Sin shall be forever banished from God's good earth (3) All prophecy shall be fulfilled (4) Righteousness and holiness shall for ever fill the earth (5) Anti-Christ with his anti-christian system shall be destroyed and God shall be all in all.

MICHAEL THE ARCHANGEL
Key:
   "He understood."
   "He had understanding of the vision." (Dan. 10:1)

10

MICHAEL THE ARCHANGEL

The time appointed was long

A close and careful reader of the Scriptures cannot fail to be impressed by the hints given here and there that the reign of Christ was to be in the far off future. In the parable of the vineyard the man who planted the vineyard and let it out to husbandmen, went into a far country, *for a long time*. The man was Jehovah, the far country was heaven, and he went into that far country FOR A LONG TIME. How long, of course is unknown and hence the necessity of WATCHING AND PRAYING. It is in God's hands to cut the time short or prolong it as He pleases. Daniel knew that the millennium was in the far away future. THE TIME APPOINTED WAS LONG. That there is a near and far fulfillment of prophecy may be clearly seen by comparing scripture with scripture. Joel's prophecy of the day of the Lord had its NEAR fulfillment on the Day of Pentecost. It shall have its more distant fulfillment after the rapture of the Church saints, when the Holy Spirit shall be poured upon all Israel and that for which Moses longed shall actually be accomplished, for all God's people shall be prophets and shall be anointed with God's Spirit. The same truth applies to the king of fierce countenance in Daniel 8. The near fulfillment of the prophecy was accomplished in Antiochus Epiphanes. The distant fulfillment awaits the apocalypse of the more desolating and destroying Anti-Christ. Daniel 10:1 throws out the hint that the complete fulfillment of these things was yet in the dim distant future. "The time appointed was long."

In the third year of Cyrus

Daniel must have been at least ninety years old when God gave him this remarkable revelation. During the reign of

Nebuchadnezzar, Belshazzar and Cyrus, Daniel lived and labored for God and His people.

I ate no pleasant bread

Self-denial is almost a lost sacrament. Daniel was not only pure in heart but temperate in life. By precept and practice Daniel prevailed.

Set me upon my knees and upon the palms of my hands

When the great God of heaven manifests himself to the saintliest of earth, comeliness turns to corruption and only one attitude befits a man in the presence of his maker. It is the attitude of a little pet dog at the feet of its master. UPON KNEES AND HANDS the Syro-Phenician woman pleaded with the Savior of men. Her attitude of humility and persistent believing prayer prevailed. Christ handed her the keys to the whole storehouse.

Stand upright

When God comes, we go down. When we go down in humility God comes closer and lifts us up. After he lifts up He gives strength to stand. The strength which he gives is intended to make us and keep us upright. The great problem of the world today as in the ages past has been the problem of sin. How shall man be healed of the plague of sin and selfishness? What shall we do? "Let him alone," growls the Atheist. "Develop him," argues the materialist. "Educate him," advises the school man. "Church him," cries the ritualist. All these human panaceas have been and are being tried and all have signally failed. Man needs a Divine power outside of himself to regenerate him and lift him up and stand him upon both of his feet and give him power to walk, run and mount up with wings as eagles. Man needs God in Christ to redeem him, save him, sanctify him wholly and keep him standing upright.

A man greatly beloved

Daniel was the beloved prophet as John later was the beloved apostle. (John 13:23) Daniel at this time was by the side of the great river Hiddekel the modern name of which is Tigris. He saw a man girded with the fine gold of Uphaz or Ophir and was informed that he was a man greatly beloved which must have greatly encouraged the prophet.

The prince of the kingdom of Persia

There are two great forces operating in our world. The empires of earth and governments of the world are controlled and their activities governed by satanic forces. Satan is the god of this age. He is also the PRINCE of the power of the air. Over each kingdom, empire, nation and republic, there is an evil-ruling prince. For three full weeks Daniel denied himself, mourned and prayed. From the first day that he set his heart to understand and to chasten himself before God in prayer and supplication, God heard his cry, and sent Gabriel to him but the evil prince of the kingdom of Persia withstood him and for twenty-one days this satanic prince hindered the answer to Daniel's prayer. Not until Michael came to Gabriel's help were the evil purposes thwarted and the prayers of Daniel answered. Had Daniel not been persistent he would not have prevailed. Gabriel and Michael fought for God and Daniel. Michael is the prince who watches over the affairs and safeguards the interests of the Hebrew race. Gabriel is the prince who is especially and peculiarly interested in the good government of God in this world and is the strong supporter and contender for righteousness in the earth. Satan, the most powerful of all the spirit intelligences is the overlord of the world, evil, and kingdom of darkness. Satan has his evil princes at strategic centres throughout the world and only by persistent prayer and faith may God's people prevail. Neither nations, presidents, monarchs nor men are free to do as they please. Gentile nations are superintended and controlled by fallen, wicked, sinful super-spirits among whom Satan is chief. The prince of the kingdom of Persia was one of these powerful agents of Satan. Too mighty for Gabriel to handle alone Michael hastened to help him. Together they prevailed and

Daniel's prayer was answered. It is instructive and awe inspiring to remember that Satan was mightier than Michael (Jude 9) and the prince of Persia more powerful than Gabriel and that the world in which we live and the air with which we are surrounded is full of fallen-spirit-intelligences bitterly engaged in opposing God, God's will and God's people.

One and twenty days

Delay is not necessarily a sign of denial.

Eph. 6:12, "For we wrestle not against flesh and blood, but against principalities, against powers, against the rulers of the darkness of this world, against spiritual wickedness in high places."

Several times in the scripture of truth the veil which separates this world from the unseen world is lifted. Satan is clearly revealed as the prince of this present evil world, the god of this age and the prince of the power of the air. Satan has his obedient subjects both in this world and in the unseen world. There is a fully organized kingdom of evil and darkness, over which Satan rules and reigns. One of Satan's lieutenants was appointed to watch over the kingdom of Persia and take care of all the interests of his satanic master. He hindered the answer to Daniel's prayer for three weeks and but for the assistance of Michael the Archangel who flew to the help of Gabriel, Daniel's prayer may never have been answered nor this important truth revealed. To show the dreadful presence and power of such diabolical intelligences it is only necessary to bear in mind that Gabriel and Michael are the most powerful of all holy angels and yet it took both of them to overcome one of Satan's lieutenants and get God's answer down to Daniel. Selah!

Michael, one of the chief princes

Michael is the only archangel mentioned in the Bible. He is Israel's generalissimo—prince—watcher. The last time his name appears is in Rev. 12, where he declares an aggressive war on Satan and casts him out of his kingdom in the heavenlies and flings him to the earth, preparatory to his arrest by Christ, and his incarceration in the bottomless pit.

Thy people

Both God and Gabriel disown the children of Israel because of their wilfullness, waywardness and wickedness. They are DANIEL'S people, not God's people. In Daniel's prayer to God he prayed THY people. In God's answer it was THY people. It is tremendously important to notice this play upon the word THY.

What shall befall thy people in the latter days

Here is an intimation clear and plain that this prophecy while describing at length the doings of Antiochus the Old Testament Anti-Christ, reaches to the concluding calamities of Israel's history through the Great Tribulation prior to their full restoration at Christ's Second Advent. Thus Antiochus Epiphanes was but a shadow of the coming Anti-Christ.

The prince of Persia

All earthly kingdoms have a reigning evil prince who acts as an agent of Satan in the affairs of government. Satan is the prince of the power of the air, the god of this age, the spirit who now works in the children of disobedience, the accuser of the brethren, and the enemy of God. He has special agents attending to his affairs, one of which was the prince of Persia. The Medo Persian Empire conquered Babylon and was in turn conquered by Greece. All Bible students should make an exhaustive study of the Satan of the Bible (1) His fall, Isa. 14:12-14 (2) His work, Luke 4:1-3, 5-7, 9 (3) His agents, Luke 8:30 (4) His Power, Job 1:14-16, 2:7, Luke 13:16, 2 Cor. 11:14, Acts 5:3 (5) His Doom, Rev. 20:10.

Who is it that stirs the nations to hatred and jealousy of other nations? Who is it that unleashes the dogs of war? Who is it that stirs up the musses and messes in Cuba? Mexico? Japan? France? Germany? There is no way to account for the hellish holocaust of 1914-18 apart from satanic subtlety and influence. No one knows who started that great war and nothing but evil resulted therefrom. Satanic princes were at the bottom of the whole baneful business. Who is it that keeps America and Japan at loggerheads? There is only one satisfactory answer. The evil prince of Japan like the evil prince of Persia and the millions of other evil princes stationed by Satan at strategic centers around the world, seek to stir up strife and sink the ships of state with all on board, into the blackness of darkness forever.

Michael your prince

Michael is the only archangel mentioned in the Bible. He is the angelic head of the Jewish people and their special angelic guardian. He contended with the devil about the body of Moses and he is to fight against Satan in defence of the Jews in the latter days (Rev. 12). He helped Gabriel against the evil prince of Persia and but for his help Daniel's prayer would have been unanswered.

THE COMING ANTI-CHRIST

11

THE COMING ANTI-CHRIST

Persia and Grecia

Here is history foretold. Four kings were to arise in Persia and four kings have come and gone and the fourth indeed was far richer than the other three as all students of history know. This prophecy also asserts that no one of Alexander's family should succeed him. Dominion was to pass from his family altogether which also has been minutely fulfilled. Judah lay right between the rival powers and Palestine became the perpetual battlefield. Nations formed alliances, intermarried, fought, bled and died just as Daniel the prophet foresaw and foretold (11:5-20).

And now will I show thee the truth

Three kings were to arise in Persia. These were (1) Cambyses (2) Smerdis (4) Darius Hystaspes. The fourth which was to be "far richer than them all" was Xerxes, who stirred up all against the empire of Greece (1-2). Alexander the Great was to oppose the Medes and Persians and rule with great dominion and do according to his own will. His kingdom however, was to be broken and divided toward the four winds of heaven (Vs. 3-4). This breaking up and dividing of the Grecian Empire was to be followed by intrigues and conflicts between the northern kingdom and the southern kingdom. For generations these two strong kingdoms fought and schemed for the mastery (Vs. 5-13). Then follows a prophetic history of the rise, wars, schemes, intrigues, diplomacies and fall of kings and people unto the time of the end, culminating in the Anti-Christ who shall do according to his own will, exalt himself, magnify himself above every god, blaspheme the God of heaven and like all materialistic, egotistic blasphemers he shall come to his end and none shall help him (15-45).

The truth

God's word is the only infallible rule of faith and practice. Every word of God is important and essential. There has been in the past and there is in the present far too much flippant talk such as: In essentials unity, In nonessentials liberty, In all things, charity. It is well to be reminded that there is no such thing as a nonessential in the Bible. Man shall not live by bread alone BUT BY EVERY WORD . . . OF GOD. Some truths may be more important than others, but ALL TRUTH IS important and ESSENTIAL.

There shall stand up yet three kings in Persia

Gabriel continues his revelation to Daniel concerning the ages to come. In the first year of Darius the Mede, Gabriel stood to confirm and strengthen Michael in the warfare in the spirit world. Gabriel arrests the attention of Daniel by affirming that he is particularly sent to shew Daniel the truth and thus answer his prayers and reward him for his devotion and piety.

In Chapter 11 the whole history of Persia is foretold and the future made known.

A mighty king

"And a mighty king shall stand up, that shall rule with great dominion, and do according to his will. And when he shall stand up, his kingdom shall be broken, and shall be divided toward the four winds of heaven; and not to his posterity, nor according to his dominion which he ruled: for his kingdom shall be plucked up, even for others beside those." This mighty king was Alexander the Great, who, after a successful career and after conquering the world, suddenly died, and his kingdom was divided toward the four winds of heaven.

His kingdom shall be broken

Here is a plain prophecy of the death of Alexander and the disruption of his empire which was to be divided into four parts under four generals. It was clearly prophesied that his sons were not to succeed him and it was just as clearly fulfilled. When he (Alexander) shall stand up, his kingdom shall be broken (defeat, disruption and division) and shall be divided toward the four winds of heaven (four rulers instead of one) and not to his posterity (his sons were not to succeed him).

His kingdom shall be plucked up, even for others besides those

The "THOSE" has reference to the four generals. The "OTHERS" sets forth in ONE word of inspiration the continuation of the Grecian empire and its constant change. The word OTHERS is true to this very day. How wonderful is the word of God!

King of the south . . . north

The interval of 400 years between the close of the Old Testament and the opening of the New Testament contains little of interest to students of the sacred scriptures. The leagues and conflicts between the kings of the South and the kings of the North with Palestine as a buffer state was all foreseen by the prophet. Following the breaking up of Babylon and the death of Belshazzar there were five political periods or eras.

1. The Persian control of Palestine for about 100 years.
2. The Græco-Macedonia rule under Alexander the Great who subjugated the Medo-Persian empire (B.C. 330).
3. The Times of the Maccabees and their futile struggles for National Independence (167-141 B.C.).
4. The wicked rule of the Priests (141-63 B.C.).
5. The Conquests by the Romans (B.C. 63).

King of the north . . . south (11:3-20)

Palestine lay right between the two rival powers of Syria and Egypt. As Belgium separates Germany and France so Judah separated Syria and Egypt. As Korea stands between Japan and Manchuria, now Manchukuo, so the land of Canaan stood as a buffer state between Syria and Egypt. The two rival powers therefore made Palestine their battlefield. They formed alliances, intermarried, schemed, planned and purposed, but all to no avail. Ever and anon Syria and Egypt were at war and the land of Judah was their battle ground.

THE KINGS OF THE SOUTH refers to the Kings of Egypt, while the expression "the kings of the north" has reference to the kings of Syria. Egypt was south of Palestine while Syria was north. Palestine was in the midst. The glorious land became the battle ground of the centuries. The long series of wars, strife, bloodshed, deceit, diplomacy and trickery depicted in Dan. 11 has been so minutely fulfilled that the critics have argued that it must have been written after the events described had actually happened. They argue that such a correct and complete history could never have been written beforehand. Blind unbelief is sure to err. We believe that God knows the end from the beginning. Prophecy is simply history written in advance as history is simply prophecy fulfilled.

And the king shall exalt himself (11:36)

Daniel jumps across the church centuries and sweeps abruptly into the Great Tribulation. Between verses 35 and 36 there is a long unreckoned period of time, during which God is calling out a Church and Bride, and which was unnoticed by the prophet Daniel. The wilful king of V. 36 is the Anti-Christ. The Jews and the world at large rejected the true Christ, the true King, who came to them in God's name. They will accept the Anti-Christ who will come in his own name (John 5:43). He will deceive the whole world, break his covenant with the Jews and desolate their land, city and temple. This *"idol shepherd,"* this *"man of the earth,"* this *"man of sin,"* this "SON OF PERDITION," this "BEAST," this "ANTI-CHRIST," this "PRINCE THAT SHALL COME," this "KING" who shall do according to his own will, this self exalting, self magnifying super-egotist, this blasphemer, this disregarder of the God of his fathers, this arch enemy of Christ, this Satan energized materialist, this desolator of desolators, this murderer and deceiver shall come to his end and none shall help him. The Lord shall consume him with the brightness of his coming.

Daniel, Paul and John with unmistakably united voice and pen, prophesy concerning the stupendous signs and scenes of the last days, the end time, the day of the Lord. Not only so, but the testimony of our Lord Jesus Christ is identical with theirs, and all together they solemnly assure us that evil will prevail and increase to the end, that wickedness will intensify and will culminate at last in the great apostasy and final revelation of the man of sin, the Anti-Christ. The many Anti-Christs of John's day and also of our own day will head up in one great Dictator of dictators, a combined Mussolini, Hitler, Stalin, Napoleon and Kemal Pasha all in one. Not only or simply a system of evil, such as Popery, Mohammedanism, Communism, Militarism, Modernism or Heathenism, but all these in one, headed by a person of such power as will make the present Pope and Pasha and the rest of earth's so called Potentates look like Pigmies.

Till the indignation be accomplished

The eleventh chapter of Daniel sets forth in graphic outline the course of Gentile power and dominion from the days of Darius (v. 1) and Alexander the Great (v. 3) down to the coming of Antiochus Epiphanes (the madman vs. 4-29) through to the great tribulation (30-35) and the apocalypse of the Anti-Christ (v. 36). The king of v. 36 is the last great enemy of God and Israel, the Anti-Christ. Daniel jumps over the present Church age in which we now live and which has already run its course for more than 1900 years and during which time God has been "calling out" a people for His own name. (The present dispensation of the Holy Spirit or Church age was not made known by Daniel).

The king of v. 36 who shall do according to his own will, exalt himself and speak marvelous things against the God of gods and prosper, is none other than the Anti-Christ. During the closing seven years of Gentile dominion and power he shall practice and prosper. He shall not regard the God of Seth, Noah, Shem, Abraham, Isaac, Jacob or Judah (his fathers) nor shall he regard the Christ of the God of his fathers (the desire of women) nor regard any god (Buddha, Confucius, Mohammed, Mason, Elk, Oddfellow, Pope, or any other god) for he shall magnify himself above all. He shall be a Hitler, Mussolini, Kemal Pasha, Lenin, Stalin, and Pope all in one. He shall honor the god of brute force and woe to those who dare to challenge his power (36-39). For seven years he shall practice and prosper TILL THE INDIGNATION BE ACCOMPLISHED. The indignation is the time of Jacob's trouble, THE TRIBULATION, THE GREAT, during which time the Anti-Christ shall be supreme.

God's fierce wrath upon Israel, hell let loose on earth, the Anti-Christ supreme, all the world at the feet of Satan and worshipping at the shrine of sin, constitute only a part of the coming tribulation or indignation.

That that is determined shall be done

To oppose, is to be like a moth against a powerful gas light. To resist is to imitate an insane man dashing his head against the walls of his cell. That that is determined shall be done.

He shall magnify himself above all

Subtle attempts are constantly being made to deify man and humanize God. The deification of man was first attempted in the garden of Eden. "Ye shall be as God" was the subtle, slimy hint of the serpent. Nimrod was the second person to start a movement which if successful would have defeated God and exalted man. "Let US build us a tower and let US make US a name lest we be scattered." God had ordered them to scatter abroad and fill the earth. Nimrod ran counter to the plans and purposes of God and brought upon himself and the race the judgments of God which resulted in the first Babel or Babylon.

Pharaoh followed Nimrod by sticking his imperialistic mailed fist under the nostrils of God and saying "Who is the Lord that I should obey him?" It was not long before he discovered the answer. In just a few days God wrapped him in a pocketless shroud. Nebuchadnezzar also attempted the deification of man and the humanization of God by making an image both excellent and terrible. He found at least three holy youths in his kingdom who would neither bow nor bend. Darius later issued an edict forbidding prayer to any God or gods except himself thus deifying man and displacing God, with the result that God delivered Daniel from the mouth of the lions. The next and last attempt to put man in the place of God will be by the Anti-Christ who will exalt himself, magnify himself ABOVE God and demand worship.

As Lucifer before he fell, and Pharaoh in his blasphemous boast before the dreadful passover night, and Nebuchadnezzar before God took away his power to reason and think, SO the Anti-Christ of coming days shall magnify himself. This is one striking characteristic in all world dictators of the past and present, whether Nebuchadnezzar, Darius, Alexander, Cæsar, Mussolini, the Pope, or Hitler, they are alike in that *they magnify themselves.*

Daniel 11:1-2 gives the prophetic history of Persia.

Daniel 11:3-20 foretells the history of Greece.

Daniel 11:21-35 sets forth the history of Israel and Israel's fierce foe during Maccabean times.

Daniel 11:36-45 forewarns the people of God of the last great monster and murderer, the Anti-Christ, the king who will be the chief enemy of God's people in coming days, who will invent a new order of worship and compel all to pay homage or perish, who will perform miracles and thus more surely deceive the multitudes and who will exalt himself above all.

Neither shall he regard the God of his fathers

The Anti-Christ shall be a God defying and Christ rejecting rebel. Here also is one proof that the Anti-Christ shall be of the Hebrew race. The expression "The God of his fathers" is always Jewish. The Anti-Christ must be a Jew. This sweeps away the idea that the Pope is or will be the Anti-Christ. Neither Kaiser Bill nor Mussolini, nor Hitler, nor Napoleon were Hebrews. Neither Cain, nor Nimrod were Jews, and the Anti-Christ must be a Jew.

The God of his fathers

The FATHERS always has reference to the Old Testament patriarchs. Seth, Shem, Abraham, Isaac, Jacob and Jacob's twelve sons were the fathers of the nation of Israel. The expression "Neither shall he regard the God of his fathers" proves beyond quibble or question that the Anti-Christ will be a Jew, and hence neither the Pope, Hitler, Mussolini, Kaiser Bill nor Roosevelt can qualify as the Anti-Christ. The coming "man of sin" will be all these in one person.

Nor the desire of women

Respect for women is swiftly disappearing from the earth. Women themselves are largely to blame. The shocking shamelessness of the present female species of the human family, with their nudity, their disgusting bathing costumes and dress, their shapeless, bony, stockingless legs, their puppy dog friendships, their lip stick and paint, their giggling, painted, deceptive curling lips and cigarette stained fingers, these and other equally disgusting practices are fast sweeping away the last vestige of respect for girls and women. The devil and the fashion fixers are swiftly destroying the one time universal respect once shown to women and girls. The expression "nor the desire of women" is very striking. All Jewish girls looked forward to becoming the honored Mother of the Messiah and hence the above words may imply that the Anti-Christ will be as his name actually implies, i. e. one who is opposed to Christ.

The God of forces

The Anti-Christ will be a great world dictator and Militarist. The next war will be a terrifying holocaust. One gas bomb dropped upon London, New York or Paris will destroy every living plant, animal and man. Irresistible forces will know no impregnable barriers or immovable objects. An American gun now in Maryland can propel a 200 lb. shell with sufficient force to penetrate through a sixteen inch armor plate. Man will be helpless before the combined forces of nature, armies, navies, death dealing machines and chemicals in the air and sea, under the sea and upon the earth.

With a strange god

Satan is even now awaiting the hour for *his* son—the son of perdition, to appear. Satan is now ready for the apocalypse of *his* man—the *man of sin*. The true and living God gave His Son to save the world and Satan is yet to give his son to damn the world. The God of heaven has given to the race His man, the ideal man, the perfect man, the man of righteousness, truth and holiness and Satan shall yet give his man, the man of sin. The *mystery of Godliness* appeared 1900 years ago to redeem the race; the *mystery of iniquity* only awaits the rapture of the saints. God's prince and King offered Himself to the world and was despised and rejected of men; Satan's prince and coming wilful king shall yet appear, be accepted and worshipped. The power of God was placed at the disposal of God's Christ and the power of Satan will be given to Satan's Anti-Christ. God's Christ came from above Satan's Anti-Christ shall come up out of the pit. Rev. 11-7 "And when they shall have finished their testimony, the beast that ascendeth out of the bottomless pit shall make war against them, and shall overcome them, and kill them." God's Christ came in His Father's name; Satan's Anti-Christ shall come in His own name. "I am come in my Father's name, and ye receive me not; if another shall come in his own name, him ye will receive" (John 5:43). God's Christ humbled himself, Satan's Anti-Christ exalts himself. "And the king shall do according to his will; and he shall exalt himself, and magnify himself above every god, and shall speak marvelous things against the God of gods, and shall prosper till the indignation be accomplished" (Dan. 11:36). God's Christ came to do His Father's will, Satan's Anti-Christ shall do according to his own will. (Dan. 11:36). God's Christ was and is *the truth*, Satan's Anti-Christ shall be the lie. "For this cause God shall send them a strong delusion that they should believe a lie" (2 Thess. 2:11). God's Christ accomplished His miracles and wonders through the power of God, Satan's Anti-Christ shall do . . . with a strange god (Dan. 11-36-39).

Whom he shall acknowledge and increase with glory

"The God of his fathers," seems to favor the idea that the *Anti-Christ* will be a Jew. "The desire of women," may refer to Christ, the Jewish Messiah. Everything in the book of Daniel is Jewish. Every Jewish maiden yearned to be honored by becoming the mother of the Messiah. *He* was the desire of women. "Whom he shall acknowledge and increase with glory" indicates clearly that the Anti-Christ will willingly worship the devil. Satan offered Christ the kingdoms of the world and that which Christ refused and rejected *Anti-Christ* will accept. As Christ sought the glory of God so the Anti-Christ shall seek the glory of his god, the devil.

The Libyans and Ethiopians shall be at his steps

For seven years Anti-Christ shall be the supreme ruler and desolating Dictator of the world. Disregarding both the will of God and His Christ, the Anti-Christ shall do according to his own will and magnify himself above God (Dan. 11:36-38). He shall oppose and exalt himself above all that is called God or that is worshipped. As God, he shall sit in the temple of God in Jerusalem and profess himself to be God, and shall practice and prosper (2 Thess. 2:1-4). All opposition will be ruthlessly dealt with, and all rebels against his reign and rule will be mercilessly mangled and destroyed. The King of the South shall push at him and the King of the North shall come against him like a whirlwind (v. 40) and Palestine shall be the centre of the titanic struggle (v. 41). The Anti-Christ for a time shall be victorious (v. 42). The wealth of the world shall be at his disposal (v. 43). The continent of Africa, the Sons of Ham, will be solidly behind him (v. 43). "The Libyans and Ethiopians" shall be at his steps." Tidings out of the East and out of the north shall trouble him for it is a time of trouble, indignation, wrath and tribulation (v. 44). Filled with the devil and supported by the Satanic spirits of hell, Anti-Christ shall go forward to destroy (v. 44) *Rule or ruin* is his devilish motto. He goes forth to devour, destroy and damn the sons of men (v. 44). He shall plant his palaces in the land of Palestine, and, Monarch of all he surveys, King of all the earth, Ruler of all the race, Supreme Dictator of the world, pope, prophet, priest of all religions, President of all mankind, everywhere, his satanic majesty, the Anti-Christ shall hold complete sway over business, commerce, politics and religion. All must receive his mark or be mercilessly mangled and slain. All must bow the knee to him or be broken.

A universal, world wide business boycott will make buying and selling impossible. Without his own peculiar SWASTIKA, NRA, *Blue eagle* or some such like mark upon the buyers and sellers, business will be impossible. Without the mark of the Anti-Christ death is sure. Just as the Anti-Christ reaches the pinnacle of his power, just when he is at the height of his unholy ambitions, he comes to his end and none shall help him (11:45). How he comes to his end is fully revealed elsewhere. The Lord Jesus Christ in flaming fire descends from heaven, arrests the Anti-Christ in person, and flings him into the lake of fire which is his final doom. The Anti-Christ will be the first person to be cast into THE LAKE OF FIRE which will be the new hell of the future (See "Riches from Revelation").

THE COMING ANTI-CHRIST / 171

The Libyans and Ethiopians

The country which the Hebrews described as "Cush" lay to the south of Egypt. The Ethiopians were well known to the Hebrews through their business intercourse with Egypt. The inhabitants of Ethiopia were of Hamitic stock (Gen. 10:6). They were divided into various tribes, of which the Sabeans or Sabæans seemed the most powerful. Their distinguished Queen once visited Solomon and is known to us as "The Queen of Sheba." These Sabeans were used by Satan to afflict Job (Job 1:15).

It was a man of Ethiopia, an eunuch of great authority, under Candace, Queen of the Ethiopians, who, having come to Jerusalem for to worship, and returning, was sitting in his chariot reading Isaiah the prophet (Acts 8:27).

The wife of Moses is described as an Ethiopian woman (Num. 12:1). Ethiopia has been brought into great prominence through the murderous machinations of the mad Fascist, Mussolini.

Between the seas in the glorious holy mountain

"The glorious holy mountain" of course is Palestine. "Between the seas" has reference to the Mediterranean sea, the sea of Galilee and the Dead Sea. Megiddo, the battle field of the ages, is truly between the seas in the glorious holy mountain. It is yet to be the mustering place of the Anti-Christ in the Holy Land. Megiddo or Armageddon is the place at which the hosts of hell, led by Satan and his Anti-Christ will finally gather (Rev. 16:16). It lies on the southern verge of the historic Plain of Esdraelon, the well known Valley of Jezreel. It is the place of the final mustering of the Anti-Christian hosts. Both Jerusalem with the valley of Jehoshaphat and Megiddo with its valley of Jezreel are truly "between the seas in the glorious holy mountain." The Hebrew word Harmageddon like the Greek word Armageddon means simply the Mount of Megiddo. The future Satanic Anti-Christ battle line is likely to extend from the plains of Megiddo south to the Valley of

Jehoshaphat and Jerusalem and farther south to the land of Edom. Satan with his Anti-Christ is yet to make his last stand and most desperate attempt to destroy God's saints. When victory seems within sight Christ descends and smites the forces of Satan and Anti-Christ and delivers his saints.

He shall come to his end

Daniel 11:36-45 is full of deep and mysterious things. The Anti-Christ will evidently be a very high minded, self willed, proud, arrogant, idolatrous, covetous, wicked, materialistic-blasphemer. As Satan, Pharaoh, Nimrod, and others before him he shall do according to his own will. As Lucifer, Nebuchadnezzar and Herod, he shall exalt himself and magnify himself. He shall speak against the God of the Hebrews and for a time shall prosper (Dan. 11:36). The king of the south and the king of the north however shall oppose his will for a time and terrible will be the clash of arms. Dreadful days indeed! No wonder such times are called THE TRIBULATION THE GREAT (Dan. 11:36-45 and 12:1).

The Anti-Christ and False Prophet are to be arrested by Christ and summarily destroyed by being flung alive into the lake of fire. As Enoch and Elijah were taken to heaven without dying so the Anti-Christ and the false prophet will be cast alive into the lake of fire.

THE CLOSING SCENES AND SIGNS OF THE TIMES

"The world's midnight is yet to come. That was a dark day when the flood swept the antediluvian world into the pit. It was a dreadful day when the fiery billows rolled over the fair plains of Sodom and Gomorrah. It was a sad day when Pharaoh put his heel upon the Israelitish heart in the dark night of Egyptian bondage. The fall of Jerusalem and the Babylonish captivity was a severe stroke, but far worse was that of the siege of Jerusalem under Titus, when mothers ate the flesh of their own dead children, and untold horrors reigned supreme. Fire and flood, war, pestilence, and famine, have all contributed their dark chapters to the world's history. But . . . there is an awful time coming, the darkness of which will overshadow all the tempestuous epochs of the past, and might very appropriately be termed the world's midnight."

REV. J. O. MCCLURKAN.

12

THE CLOSING SCENES

At that time

In order to clearly understand Daniel 12 the reader should compare it with Revelation 12. These two chapters make it clear that there are to be *special* and *separate resurrections* for certain of the Jews and Israelites, at specific periods during the seven years Great Tribulation. If the reader will remember that Daniel 12 is still speaking of "thy people" i. e. Daniel's people, he will clearly perceive and understand such scriptures as "many of them that sleep . . . shall awake." It is not so much the fact of a resurrection which is occupying the attention of the Prophet for ALL who sleep in the dust shall eventually awake. Daniel is thinking and writing about special, separate and specific awakenings or resurrections of God's people during the Great Tribulation. Daniel 12:1 has nothing whatever to do with either the Gentiles or the Church for it plainly applies only to Daniel's people. "Thy people" twice mentioned in the verse refers ONLY to Daniel's people. There is to be an *out resurrection* for the special elect remnant of Israel during the Great Tribulation as there is to be a special select OUT RESURRECTION FROM THE DEAD of all the Church saints at the second appearing of Christ at the close of this Church age. Not only is there to be a future NATIONAL RESURRECTION of Israel but there is also to be a special, select OUT RESURRECTION of the faithful martyred remnant during the Great Tribulation.

"At that time" refers to the time during which the wilfull king, or Anti-Christ oppresses the Jews. "At that time," the time of his apparent greatest triumph—*at that time*—shall Michael, the Archangel, stand up in defense of God's people. Michael is Israel's special prince and defender.

There shall be a time of trouble

"For then shall be great tribulation, such as was not since the beginning of the world to this time, no, nor ever shall be" (Matt. 24:21).

"For when they shall say, Peace and safety, then sudden destruction cometh upon them, as travail upon a woman with child; and they shall not escape" (I Thess. 5:3).

"And at that time shall Michael stand up, the great prince which standeth for the children of thy people; and there shall be a time of trouble, such as never was since there was a nation even to that same time: and at that time thy people shall be delivered, every one that shall be found written in the book" (Daniel 12:1).

"For, behold, the Lord cometh out of his place to punish the inhabitants of the earth for their iniquity: the earth also shall disclose her blood, and shall no more cover her slain"

1. It will be a time of Judgment on Apostate Christendom.
2. It will be a period of special desolation.
3. It will be an era of dreadful wickedness.

(Isa. 26:21).

4. Anti-Christ will be world dictator.
5. The False Prophet will complete the Trinity of hell (1) Satan (2) Anti-Christ (3) False Prophet.
6. It will be a time of trouble, such as never was (Dan. 12:1).

At that time thy people shall be delivered

Israel may be likened to an EXCURSION which is delayed, sidetracked, or held up in a siding, and waiting for the EXPRESS which is the Church, and which now has right of way. Church truth was not revealed by Daniel. The Church age was not opened to the vision of the Prophet. The mystery of the Church's birth, growth, glory, rapture and return to the earth was revealed to the Apostle of the Gentiles, and not by Daniel the Prophet. The expression THY PEOPLE refers to Daniel's people i e. the Jew.

Shall Awake

The literal, bodily Resurrection of Christ is the corner stone of Christian Doctrine. It is also the Gibraltar of Christian Evidence, the Waterloo of Infidelity and the sure and certain proof that the saints shall also awake in his likeness some glad and glorious day.

If there is no resurrection of the dead, then, faith is vain, we are all sinners and false witnesses. Christ is also dead. (1 Cor. 15:13-17) and the race is doomed. We need to be reminded that if Christ did not arise from the dead, mankind is lost and salvation and heaven are alike impossible.

Many of them that sleep . . . shall awake:

Daniel had just been informed that the great prince Michael shall stand up to defend God's cause and God's people (Dan. 12:1, Rev. 12), that the "Agony of the ages" was yet in the future, and that the faithful remnant would be preserved through the fiery furnace of that coming agony. The words "many of them" have to do with Daniel's people. The "them" of v. 2 refers to the "thy people" of v. 1 and has nothing to do with the Gentiles or a so-called general resurrection. There is no such thing known to the scriptures as a GENERAL resurrection. The resurrections of which the Bible speaks are all ear-marked, special, select resurrections. Beginning with MOSES and continuing with THE WIDOW'S SON, LAZARUS, CHRIST, DORCAS, the *saints* who arose with Christ, the coming rapture of the living and resurrection of the sleeping *saints* at the coming of the Lord, the national resurrection of Israel and their restoration to their own land just prior to the setting up of the millennium, the resurrection of *saints* during the great tribulation, *and last,* the resurrection of all *the wicked dead* at the close of the millennium (Rev. 20: 11-15) they are each and all earmarked resurrections. A general resurrection of sinners and saints at the end of the world is utterly foreign to the Scriptures. "Many of them that sleep . . . shall awake" has reference *only* to Jews—thy people—

Daniel's people (v. 1). Not only is there to be a national resurrection of all Israel such as was seen by Ezekiel in his vision of the dry, yes! very dry bones (Ezekiel 37), but there is to be a special resurrection of Jewish Saints who suffered martyrdom during the great tribulation and the cruel reign of the Anti-Christ. Such special saints are marked out for a special resurrection to everlasting life and participation with Christ in his glorious millennial kingdom. Not only are the faithful few, who, rather than disobey, suffered and died, to arise from the dead during the closing scenes of the great tribulation, but those who received the mark of the beast, those apostate Jews who bowed before the image of the Anti-Christ and received his mark, they, too, are to arise from the dead only to be covered with shame and everlasting contempt. Special sinners are marked out for special shame!

Some to everlasting life

The *some* here refers to the Jewish Saints during the great tribulation who elected to die rather than yield. There will be Daniels, who, rather than stop praying will suffer themselves to be slain. There will be Hananiahs, Mishaels and Azariahs, who, rather than bow down to the image set up by the Anti-Christ will suffer themselves to be slaughtered. Such, who sleep in the dust of the earth shall awake as a special resurrected company and thus inherit everlasting life.

Some to shame and everlasting contempt

The *SOME* in this passage has reference to those of the children of Abraham who during the fearful hours of the great tribulation became like Judas, Demas and Ananias, who received the mark of the beast, and as special sinners shall awake to special shame and contempt. Daniel 11 and 12 thus deals with all history from the first year of Darius the Mede to the closing scenes of the oncoming Great Tribulation, the apocalypse of the Anti-Christ and the ushering in of God's Utopian morning that shall know no night.

Everlasting contempt

Everlasting contempt. What terrible words! Two classes are here dealt with by the prophet (1) Those who accept the truth and despite the terrible trials and persecutions through which they are called upon to pass, and despite the fact that they must suffer martyrdom for their faith, endure as seeing Him who is invisible and consequently awake to everlasting life. (2) Those who accept the false Messiah who comes in his own name, and who receive his mark. Those who submit rather than suffer. Those who yield rather than endure. Such shall also awake but to shame and eternal contempt. During the dreadful days of the Great Tribulation there is a special reward for special faithfulness and a special shame for special sin.

They that be wise

Better be wise than be wealthy. A half witted boy watching the funeral of a once wealthy miser remarked, "There he goes and not a penny in his pocket."

The word here translated WISE is the word used for INSTRUCTORS OR TEACHERS of others. It means wise in the sense of conveying the truth to others. Those who know the truth of God and *instruct others therein* shall shine as the brightness of the firmament.

They that turn many to righteousness

Those who have been burning and shining lights, those who have instructed others, those who have been fishers of men, those who have been, in season and out of season, saviors of sinners and seekers for souls shall enjoy glorious reward. What an incentive to soul winning! "They that be teachers shall shine as the brightness of the firmament and they that turn many to righteousness as the stars forever and ever."

Shut up the words and seal the book

If these were the closing words of the book of Daniel, as some have preached and practiced by severely leaving the contents of the book alone, we might well despair of ever understanding its meaning. We may thank God, however, that such is not the closing word. There is no full stop after the words *SEAL THE BOOK*, for the whole passage reads "Shut up the words ... seal the book, to the time of the end." The first book of the New Testament, the Gospel according to Matthew together with the last book of the New Testament, the Revelation according to St. John on the Isle of Patmos supplies the double key which unseals the book of Daniel. That which was sealed by Jehovah in the Old Testament is unsealed by the Holy Spirit in the New Testament.

Many shall run to and fro

"Ye hypocrites," said Jesus one day, "Ye can discern the face of the sky, but can ye not discern the signs of the times?" Nahum evidently foresaw the automobile age when he wrote, "The chariots shall be with flaming torches," and also forewarned that such would be "in the day of His Preparation." Who ever heard of raging chariots before the automobile arrived? The prophet Nahum also mentioned the principal street along which they would run and jostle one against another. "They shall jostle one another *in the broad ways.*" THE BROADWAYS of New York, Chicago, Los Angeles, San Francisco and London. These are only a few of the signs of the times (See 2 Tim. 3:1-3, Nahum 2:3-4). Nahum saw the automobile age while Daniel foretold THE AGE OF TRAVEL. "Many shall run to and fro."

"Many shall run ... and knowledge ... increased," find special fulfillment and emphasis in the present century. Railways, steam engines, steam and motor vessels, automobiles, telephones, wireless, libraries, books, newspapers, magazines, microscopes, submarines and X-rays are only a few of the inventions and discoveries of our own day and age. The prophet said "Many shall run," and many are indeed running. He said "knowledge shall be increased" and knowledge has been and is being increased.

Many shall be purified

Here is one more outstanding sign of the Times. "Many shall be purified and made white." THERE is a striking and interesting passage in the book of Hebrews which says "Some must enter therein" (Heb. 4:6). Put these two scriptures together and you have a most interesting and instructive combination (1) "Many shall" and (2) "Some must." Reverse the order and you have (1) "Some must" and (2) "Many shall." "Some must enter therein" for God's plans and purposes must be fulfilled, despite the opposition of men and devils. Thank God "Many shall be purified and made white and tried." With pure hearts (purified) and clean hands (made white) they shall thus be prepared for the fiery trials and tests of the closing days of this age.

The wicked shall do wickedly

(1) Yes! the days in which we live are the most wonderful that the world has ever seen. (2) No! the world is *not* getting better every day. (3) Yes! we are living in the midst of dreadful days. (4) Yes! the world is getting worse and worse. Evil is today a thousand times worse than it ever was. Sin is more subtle today, more devilish, more refined, and hence a thousand times more dangerous and more damnable. On the other hand there are more good and holy people in the world today than ever before in history, and goodness and truth is more abounding than ever before. The human race is on the increase. Sin and error also are on the increase and hell is being enlarged. Holiness, truth and goodness are abounding as never before. Soon or later there will be a final clash between the two forces, one of which will be headed up in the Anti-Christ and the other in God's Christ. "The wicked shall do wickedly" but "Many shall be purified and made white." When the world's cup of iniquity is full, the crises will have been reached and the smiting stone will fall, the colossus of man's day will crash and crumble, sin will forever be swept from the earth and *the*

stone, the *smiting stone,* the *stone* cut out without hands, the stone which was once set at naught, *the stone* against which Israel stumbled and was broken, *the stone* will roll on, and on, and on, gathering momentum as it rolls, until it fills the whole earth. THEN and not till then will right be on the throne and wrong be on the scaffold. THEN and not till then shall HOLINESS be triumphant and God's will be done in earth as it is done in heaven.

Daniel 12:10 describes the normal state of society from Daniel's day until the second advent of Christ. (1) Many shall be purified and made white (2) The wicked shall do wickedly (3) None of the wicked shall understand (4) The wise shall understand. So much, at least, is settled. These things are no longer open for debate, for God has spoken. The sacred scriptures never hint the gradual conversion of the world. There can never be any reconciliation of good and evil. There never can be friendship between holiness and sin. They ARE enmity. They are mutually antagonistic and destructive. The crisis will be reached when the Christ of glory comes and the Colossus of man's civilization, pomp and power crashes and crumbles to pieces. This is the end of man's day. Selah!

The abomination that maketh desolate

The expression, "the abomination that maketh desolate" is twice mentioned in the Book of Daniel and once referred to by our Lord Jesus Christ. (Cp. Dan. 11:31; Dan. 12:11; Matt. 24:15).

In Dan. 11:31 it has reference to Antiochus Epiphanes. Because of his wild, wicked, and wilful ways, words and works, he was called "Epimanes" which means "the madman." He was a forerunner and perhaps the most outstanding type of the Anti-Christ who is yet to come.

In Dan. 12:11 the expression "the abomination of desolation" refers to the Anti-Christ of whom Antiochus Epiphanes was but a type. Before our blessed Lord comes in glory at the close of the great tribulation Anti-Christ will devastate the land of promise and attempt the utter annihilation of God's people. He will declare himself to be God, demand worship, enter the temple dedicated to the God of the Hebrews, profane God's Holy things, persecute God's holy people, and attempt the extermination of all worshippers of the true and living God. He will be the climax and culmination of all wickedness, and shall be destroyed by Christ when He returns with His Saints to set up His Glorious Millennial Kingdom.

The "abomination" of Daniel 11:31 is past while the "abomination" of Dan. 12:11 is future.

The 1335 days (12:12)

The twelfth chapter of Daniel introduces us again to Michael, the only archangel mentioned in the Bible. He is the great prince, who, with Gabriel has charge of the government of God for this world. Michael and Gabriel take care of God's interests on the earth. Michael is the great prince watching over God's people, Israel, while Gabriel is chiefly concerned with the Gentiles. During the great tribulation, which is yet future, Michael shall stand up in defense of the Jews in order to preserve the faithful remnant alive in those dreadful days (Read Rev. 12 and see Riches from Revelation). The Great Tribulation will occupy the last week of Daniel's seventieth week which equals seven years. The first half of the seven years will be taken up by wars, famines, earthquakes and pestilences upon all the earth. The second half of the seven years will witness the rise of the Anti-Christ and the closing half of THE GREAT TRIBULATION proper shall begin in earnest. This will last for a time (1 year) times (2 years) and half a time (½ year) or 1260 days. At the close of the 1260 days of hell on earth, under the sovereign sway of Satan, the Anti-Christ and false prophet who constitute the trinity of hell, Christ Jesus will descend in all his eternal power and glory, arrest the devil and incarcerate him in the bottomless pit for a 1000 years, seize the Anti-Christ and fling him into the lake of fire which is his final doom. The wicked followers of Anti-Christ will be destroyed and the way cleared for the setting up of the millennial kingdom. The living nations shall be judged by Christ according to Matt. 25:31-46. The earth shall be cleaned up, the wicked nations destroyed and the way prepared for the glorious reign of Christ. This preparing of the way of the Lord will occupy 75 days and then full blessing comes to Israel, Judah and the world. The millennial reign of Christ will begin and hence "blessed he that cometh to the thousand three hundred and five and thirty days." Seventy-five days, in which the living nations shall be gathered together before the King of kings to be judged as nations, the earth swept clean and the way prepared for the glorious reign of Christ. Full blessing shall then come to Jew and Gentile and the 1000 years reign of Christ will begin.

1260 ... 1290 ... 1335 days

Here are three periods of days. (1) 1260 days or the closing half of the Great Tribulation. (2) 1290 days or 30 days before the middle of the Great Tribulation the daily sacrifice shall be taken away and the worst half of the Tribulation shall begin. (3) 1335 days or 75 days after the destruction of the Anti-Christ the full blessing of Christ's Millennium kingdom will be realized. After the smashing of the image of the Beast and the destruction of the Anti-Christ it will take 75 days to clear away the debris before the millennial kingdom of Christ is set up.

Thou shalt rest

The Bible reveals to me A FATHER, who has numbered the hairs of my head; A SAVIOR, who by his own shed blood has saved me from sin and a HEAVEN in which I am to REST in everlasting fellowship with God. GO AND REST. Daniel must have lived to a ripe old age. He must have been a very aged man when the gracious Lord told him to go and rest. He was taken captive in the 3rd year of Jehoiakim, he lived through the 70 years captivity and until the reign of Cyrus. "Go and Rest." To the saint death is but a sleep. To the Child of God the waiting time between death and resurrection is a RESTING time.

Toil and trouble, discouragements and disappointments will all be over. Daniel's long, strange, wonderful journey was about to end. No more shall he be the target for cruel, envious, jealous office seekers. He has seen his last den of hungry lions. His righteous soul shall no longer be vexed by the sin of Jew or Gentile. A good man, full of the Holy Ghost and faith, tested and true, loving and loyal, faithful and fearless, Daniel shall rest and await the resurrection morning when he shall be richly rewarded by his wonderful Redeemer and King. When our work is done, may we, too, hear the wonderful words of our wonderful Lord, "GO AND REST."

Thou shalt stand in thy lot at the end of the days

Heaven is a place as well as a state. It is a place of holy, restful activity. Nothing short of Heaven can satisfy the universal longing of humans for perfect rest, perfect knowledge, perfect God-likeness and perfect service. "Go . . . rest . . . and stand" were God's last words to his faithful prophet. Heaven and immortality are thus realities of Revelation. JOB knew that his Redeemer was alive and that after worms had banqueted on his body he knew that he would see God (Job. 19:25-27). CHRIST declared that God was the God of the living and thus assures us that Abraham, Isaac and Jacob are living (Matt. 22:32). *Lazarus'* body was probably on the ashheap or junk pile but the rich man saw him in Abraham's bosom (Luke 16). MOSES AND ELIJAH talked with Christ a 1000 years after their earthly ministries ceased (Matt. 17:3-4). Paul knew that he had a building eternal in the heavens (2 Cor. 5:1) and triumphantly declared that death would be swallowed up (1 Cor. 15:52-55).